Mercedes-Benz Diesel Automobiles

Books by W. Robert Nitske

The Amazing Porsche and Volkswagen Story was published in 1958.

The Complete Mercedes Story was first published by the Macmillan Company in 1955.

Rudolf Diesel, Pioneer of the Age of Power (with Charles M. Wilson) was published by the University of Oklahoma Press in 1965.

The Life of Wilhelm Conrad Röntgen, Discoverer of the X-Ray, was published by the University of Arizona Press in 1971.

Travels in North America, 1822-1824, a translation of the important exploration diary of Duke Paul Wilhelm of Württemberg, was published by the University of Oklahoma Press in 1973.

Mercedes-Benz 300SL was published by Motorbooks International in 1974.

The Zepplin Story was published by A. S. Barnes & Company in 1977.

Mercedes-Benz Production Models 1946-1975 was published by Motorbooks International in 1977.

Mercedes-Benz: A History was published by Motorbooks International in 1978.

Mercedes-Benz: Diesel Automobiles was published by Motorbooks International in 1981.

MERCEDES-BENZ

DIESEL
AUTOMOBILES

From the 260D of 1936 to the 300SD of 1981

by W. Robert Nitske

World-wide distributors

Motorbooks International
Publishers & Wholesalers Inc
Osceola, Wisconsin 54020, USA

First Printing

*All Illustrations, except where noted, are from
the archives of Daimler-Benz A.G.*

Book design by Harrison Shaffer

Cover design by Stanley G. Fabe

Printed by Shandling Lithographing Co., Inc.
Tucson, Arizona 85705

Library of Congress Cataloging in Publication Data

Nitske, W. Robert
    Mercedes-Benz : diesel automobiles.

        1. Mercedes automobile.   2. Automobiles—Motors
(Diesel)   I. Title.
TL215.M4N516   629.2'222   81-9605
ISBN 0-87938-146-9   AACR2

World-wide distributors
Motorbooks International, Osceola, Wisconsin, U.S.A.

Contents

Preface   vii

The Rudolf Diesel Story   1

Early Vehicular Diesel Engines   19

Mercedes-Benz Diesel Automobiles   39

380 tests   41

Model 260D   43

Model 170D   49

Model 180D   56

Mediterranée-Le Cap Rallye   62

Model 190D   66

Model 200D   71

Model 220D   76

Model 240D   84

Model 300D   94

Records for Turbocharged Diesels   102

Records for Marathon Mileage Misers   108

Model 300CD   112

Model 300SD   116

Models 240TD and 300TD   126

The GD Vehicles   134

Principles of Diesel Engines   137

Pollution and Emission Controls   145

Acknowledgements   151

Preface

In this book, the tireless efforts of the inventor Rudolf Diesel to perfect his engine are described, followed by the modification and its practical application of that type engine to passenger cars by Daimler-Benz engineers. This development eventually resulted in the line of diesel-engined models, from the relatively uncomplicated 260D of 1936 and the 170D of 1946 to the ultimate, sophisticated turbocharged 300SD of 1977.

The ever increasing popularity of diesel-engined automobiles built by Daimler-Benz is reflected in the production figures of the manufacturer, despite some evident disadvantages over the gasoline-engined cars.

The initial purchase price difference between diesel- and gasoline-powered cars showed still a disadvantageous comparison in 1980. As an example, the 200D sedan sold in Germany for about 5 percent more than the 200 model (DM 22,159 and DM 21,040). However, performance comparison told a dissimilar story. While the acceleration of 0 to 100 kilometers per hour was 16.7 seconds for the 94-horsepower 200 against 26.6 for the 60-horsepower diesel, and maximum speeds were 165 kilometers against 140 kilometers per hour, fuel consumption figures were vastly in favor of the diesel-engined model. In city driving the 200D used 9.8 liters against 14.8 liters and highway driving at 90 kilometers per hour 7.4 against 8.5, and at 120 kilometers per hour 11.0 against 11.2, for an average consumption of 9.4 liters per 100 kilometers

(24.5 miles per gallon) for the 200D and 11.5 liters (20.4 miles per gallon) for the 200 model.

In these times when the fuel situation is most critical, it is well to remember that diesel fuel has about 11 percent more energy per gallon than regular gasoline and 9 percent more than premium. And the production of diesel fuel is a considerably easier process. It has been estimated that actually five times as much energy is needed to produce gasoline than diesel fuel.

The turbocharging process gives the diesel engine a fantastic advantage over the regularly aspirated engine, furnishing more power at an even lower fuel consumption—a truly ideal solution to the fuel crisis.

Having owned, albeit briefly, two 300D sedans (a 1975 and a 1977 model), this writer now drives a 300CD (1980 model) and feels quite comfortable with the diesel. (It is, alas, no 300SL, but such spectacular cars do not happen more than once in a fortunate lifetime, and mine was so blessed.) The improvements made over the years are truly unbelievable, when compared to the horrible noise, especially when starting, the 180D made we drove in Berlin in 1956. The 1980 model runs remarkably quiet. But then, of course, within the last twenty-five years enormous refinements have been made in all types of automobiles.

Surely, the evidence supports overwhelmingly the conviction that the diesel engine has still a spectacular future, although it has been used in passenger cars successfully for over forty-five years.

Rudolf Diesel
1858-1913

The Rudolf Diesel Story

The inventor of the engine that bears his name was born Rudolf Christian Karl Diesel in 1858.

His parents lived at that time in Paris where the father, Theodor Diesel, was a maroquinier, a craftsman in leather work. The family had originally come from Augsburg, Bavaria, but were actually more Swabian, a traditionally thrifty, astute, enterprising and tough people, rather than the free-spirited Bavarian who were merry and looked upon life joyously.

Further back in history, the earliest ancestors had settled in Thuringia where the name Diesel first appeared in 1726 in official records. Ancestors of Rudolf were butchers and tradesmen, then one was a minor government employee at the Duke of Württemberg in Lugwigsburg, (then) the capital of the realm. His son, in turn, became a bookseller and small publisher in Memmingen, near Ulm, and the son and heir remained in that trade. But the next generation Diesel, Theodor, was dissatisfied to remain in the city of Augsburg where he had moved to and in 1850 this fourth-generation leather craftsman with his brother Rudolf went to Paris.

The French capital was not the gay and happy haven of song and story to the two immigrants and after considerable hardship the brother, defeated and discouraged, returned to the more familiar and hospitable Augsburg, while Theodor stubbornly held out, determined to make his living in his newly chosen environment.

Theodor met another ex-patriate, Elise Strobel, a young governess who had also settled in Paris after a short stay in England after her parents had died in Augsburg. Theodor and Elise were married, going to London for the ceremony. They had three children, Louise, Rudolf, and Emma.

Then, the business of the maroquinier expanded and at times six workmen and two apprentices worked in the "studio" to manufacture embossed leather portfolios, desk sets, pocket books, picture frames, and similar goods. Rudolf grew up in those busy surroundings.

The youngster found all sorts of interesting but not necessarily constructive activities to pass the time. He never played with other children, but amused himself in investigating such things as the inner workings of the priced cuckoo clock which he was able to take apart but unable to reassemble again. At one time he opened the gas jets in the room, but a disaster was fortunately avoided by the alertness of one of the journeymen working there. His father took a dim view of such activities and punishment was duly administered with, of course, a leather strap, to the young Rudolf.

In the Protestant School which he and his sisters attended, Rudolf showed exceptional ability. Most of the time he led his class. His drawing was excellent and the other schoolwork so superior to his fellow pupils that he was awarded at the age of twelve a bronze medal from the Société pour l'Instruction Élémentaire.

In his youth, Rudolf had the appearance of a beautiful boy, seemed incredibly wise and behaved like a poet. He was a dreamer. He made drawings and scribbled in his notebooks, after seeking solitude in the attic or some remote corner of the hallway. He frequently visited museums, especially the Conservatoire des Arts et Métiers, the oldest technical museum nearby in the Boulevard Sebastopol. Once the abbey of Saint Martin, the ancient dank and dingy edifice was crammed with dusty and oddly contrasting exhibits, all sorts of tools, models of early ships, and early steam engines. Each attracted and intrigued the young boy.

Of special delight and a magnet of interest was the original of the very first self-propelled vehicle known to history, the three-wheeled steam tractor, designed and built in 1770 by Captain Nicolas Joseph Cugnot. A round steam boiler was mounted on iron-shod wooden wheels and this contraption had actually run under its own power a hundred years before and as the guidebook stated at about two miles per hour, the speed of an ox team. But every hundred yards or so it needed to halt to build up more steam. The French Army had used the captain's invention to haul a cannon, but he vehicle had been unmanageable and ran into a stone wall. The sturdy wall was demolished and the more robust mechanical apparatus slightly damaged, but the military was reluctant to put it into regular service. Artillery pieces were hauled henceforth again by horsepower. The precocious Rudolf drew pictures of the museum's piece in his notebook.

The ever increasing hostility prevailing at that time in France against Germans under Napoleon III caused extreme hardships on Theodor Diesel, his family and his business. When Rudolf, in 1870, was to enter the Ecole Primaire Superieure — about junior high school — the Franco-Prussian War intervened.

In August the French armies suffered stunning and decisive defeats repeatedly until finally the entire army of 83,000 men was defeated and the Emperor captured at Sedan on September 1. It seemed the end of the war, but already in August a decree had been issued that all persons who were not citizens were to leave France within three days.

The Diesel Family took a crowded train to Rouen, then changed to another for Dieppe, and boarded a jam-packed steamship to cross the Channel for neutral England. After a miserable seven-hour trip over extremely rough water the Diesels arrived at Newhaven. Two days later they were in London. After terribly discouraging days and weeks, Theodor found work at a pound a week in a retail store and the brilliant fourteen-year old Louise taught languages and music in a private school. They scratched out a living in two small rooms with wooden boxes as furniture in a cheap apartment house in the Hoxton district.

Rudolf enrolled in a London school, but the experience was frustrating. However, the visits to the magnificent British Museum and the South Kensington Science Museum, his two favorite places, were stimulating and exciting.

News from the beleaguered Paris came that the harassed citizens used some ingenious devices to communicate with their outside friends. Balloons — the first had ascended eighty-eight years before — carried persons out of the capital across the Prussian lines whenever the wind was favorable. An airship, some 125 feet long, was being constructed to be powered by propellers turned by eight soldiers. And the Belgian Zenobe Gramme used an amazing dynamo to floodlight an area of Gennivillier from Montmartre.

The great Industrial Revolution had actually begun in England, then spread to the Continent. France got involved, but Germany showed an even greater effect of the movement. When in 1819 the King of Prussia had removed the internal customs barrier, trade between the 38 independent states had been boosted tremendously. In 1810 Friedrich Krupp had bought a small forge in Essen, and in 1837 Emanuel Borsig founded a machine shop in Berlin. In 1847 Werner Siemens opened a repair shop for telegraphy apparatus in Berlin and soon built a telegraph line to Frankfurt for the government. They had all become leading industrialists in Germany.

The combining of the primitive piston engine of Denis Papin and the steam boiler of Thomas Savery by Thomas Newcomen in about 1705 was perfected by James Watts and patented in 1769. But it was not until years later when Matthew Boulton manufactured such power producing machines for industrial uses that steam engines came into general use and changed the old order of manual labor.

The first train pulled by a steam engine in the United States ran from Albany to Schenectady in 1831. In Germany, the line from Fürth to Nürnberg was opened in 1835. By 1850 rails covered 3,633 miles. In Prussia alone, by 1860 that mileage totaled 6,890.

When in 1707 Denis Papin demonstrated his steam engine pulling a boat on the Fulda Kanal at Kassel, angry boatmen, fearful of losing their livelihood, ran him off and destroyed his model boat. But the Virginian mechanic James Rumsey demonstrated successfully his steamboat on the Potomac River in 1786 and four years later John Fitch carried passengers on his propeller-driven steamboat. In 1807 Robert Fulton traveled with his *Clermont* on the Hudson the 150 miles from New York to Albany in thirty-two hours.

By 1819, when the *Savannah* sailed across the Atlantic Ocean in 25 days, the steamship was well established. And in 1839 the majestic

Great Western, using 36 tons of coal daily, crossed the Atlantic in only fifteen days and started the Cunard Steamship Line in business.

The Suez Canal had just been completed when Rudolf Diesel came to London. Here in England he learned about the power available from electricity. The experiments of Benjamin Franklin were illustrated, and school books told of the discovery of the theory of the magnetic field by Johann Seebeck and the law of electrodynamics by André Ampère.

The telegraph message by Carl Steinhill from Munich to Bogenhausen in 1837 preceded the Samuel Morse message from Washington to Baltimore in 1844 and the agonies of laying an under-ocean cable by Cyrus Field.

But of all of these marvels of specacular inventions, of the greatest interest to the young Rudolf Diesel was the history of the internal combustion engine.

Christian Huygens, a Dutch astronomer had in 1680 placed a gunpowder charge into a cylinder to move a piston and develop power. The Englishmen Barnett and Clerk patented a two-stroke cycle engine but the Frenchman Jean Lenoir built the first real practical internal combustion engine, using illuminating gas as fuel. Alfonse de Rochas correctly stated the principles of the four-stroke cycle engine. But the German Nikolaus Otto and Eugen Lange actually perfected and constructed a useful engine in 1876.

The life in London was still very difficult for the Diesel family and reluctantly Rudolf was sent to Germany to study. The husband of a cousin offered to keep the boy in the Augsburg home and look after him. Professor Christoph Barnickel and his wife Betty received the young, but completely exhausted, traveler after his eight-day journey from London. He had taken a steamer from Harwich to Rotterdam, then a train to Emmerich, changed at Cologne, Frankfurt, and finally Würzburg. It was quite an experience for the twelve-year old student.

The time spent in Augsburg was a happy and fruitful period. The five years in this old city, then slowly emerging from a town of textile mills, which benefited from the water wheels built on the Lech and Wertach rivers and canals, into quite an industrial center with machine manufacturing plants. The factory of the engineer Ludwig Reichenbach, established in 1844, was an outstanding example. In fact, even the printing enterprise of the Freiherr von Cotta had a steam engine installed to furnish power to its presses.

Three technical schools had been combined in 1864 to form the Technical High School, but Rudolf had to attend a trade school first. Located in a former cloister, the building also housed a truly superb art gallery with magnificent paintings of many old masters. The school had an excellently equipped chemical laboratory and regular workshop with lathes and hearth and all manner of mechanical devices. Rudolf enjoyed the textbook studies and the practical schooling.

When he was fourteen years old he decided to become an engineer. His parents had by then returned to Paris, after the war was over, but Rudolf remained in Augsburg. He finished the trade school at the head of his class, but his parents did not want him to go to the Technical Highschool for further studies. To discuss this problem Rudolf went to Paris to see them. The 300-mile journey took forty-two hours.

While visiting with his parents, his sister Louise died suddenly. Rudolf was deeply shaken by this unexpected loss. Without convincing his parents that he ought to further his academic education, but achieving at least a concession that he may continue, Rudolf returned to Augsburg and to school to study mechanical engineering in the mechanical-technical division. Physics, mathematics, and mechanical drawing were his favorite studies. In the physics laboratory was a pneumatic fire apparatus, built like a bicycle pump. Through the glass barrel he could watch the process of compressed air igniting a spark at the end of the cylinder when the plunger was pushed down hard. It fascinated the student immensely.

The eighteen-year old Rudolf graduated as the youngest student and made the best grades ever recorded in that school. He got an "excellent" in eleven of the twelve subjects.

His excellence got him a double scholarship at the Polytechnic University in Munich, and he earned extra money by teaching French to his fellow students. His diligent studying was rewarded with the highest grade in every subject he took.

Rudolf received his German citizenship at the age of nineteen but was declared unfit for the compulsory military service because of an aggravated asthma condition.

In the Polytechnikum Rudolf was fortunate to hear lectures by Carl von Linde on heat and refrigeration machines. When this renown professor told his class that steam engines used effectively only six to ten percent of the heat energy produced, he made a notation in his notebook: "study the possibility of practical development of the isotherm." The lecture on thermodynamics was probably the spark that started Rudolf Diesel thinking of the engine he was later to build. He filled notebooks with statements of energy production and added questions: "How can this be improved?" He investigated minutely the process used by Sadi Carnot and questioned each step that the French scientist had taken in propounding the theory of a perfect engine cycle.

For the important final examination Rudolf was unable to appear. He had contacted typhus and was forced to stay in bed, but the school authorities allowed him to take his examination the next January when he had sufficiently recovered. He got the highest marks in the ten-year history of the Polytechnikum.

Through the influence of Professor von Linde, Rudolf got a position in the Sulzer factory in Winterthur, Switzerland, where also Linde refrigeration machines were built.

The Sulzer Maschinenfabrik employed three hundred men and was one of the largest and most prestigious machine building establishments in Europe. It was an excellent place for a mechanical engineering student to grow into a mechanical engineer.

Rudolf lived with fellow engineers in a factory-side rooming house and wearing the blue cotton twill coveralls of the workers, became one of them. He worked on lathes and drill presses and thoroughly mastered the other complex machinery at the huge plant.

In March 1880, Rudolf was sent to Paris to assist in the establishment of a new refrigeration plant. In a year he was the plant manager at a salary of 200 francs. When the factory was sold, Rudolf Diesel acquired the sales rights for France and Belgium. He sold and installed these machines and supervised their operation. He also found time to construct an ammonia engine and invented a process to freeze clear ice in bottles and jars. A patent for carafes frappés transparentes was issued on September 24, 1881 to him, and one for clear ice a month later.

Several ice making machines, built in Augsburg, were sold to breweries, but the inventor did not receive any cash rewards because he had been employed by von Linde at the time the process was patented.

At a party of friends Rudolf met the blond governess Martha Flasche, whom he married in Munich in November, 1883. A year later their son Rudolf was born, and in October, 1885, a daughter Hedy. In May, 1889, their second son Eugen joined the happy family.

Courtesy Deutsches Museum, Munich

Rudolf Diesel and Martha Flasche married in 1883

Diesel worked on perfecting his ammonia engine, employing three men in a rented shop, but that work did not result in a machine free of problems. The nasty gas would escape frequently and cause great concern endangering workers and the shop. Diesel had hoped to exhibit his engine at the Great Universal Exhibition, but showed the Linde ice machines only. Steam engines and internal combustion engines using illuminating gas as fuel as well as a three-wheeled Benz-Motorwagen and a tram car of Daimler's, their four stroke engines using refined gasoline, were shown. More than 28 million persons visited the Fair.

With the anti-German attitude prevailing in France, Rudolf Diesel and his family prudently moved to Germany to live and work. He was able to secure the sales rights to the Linde machines for the northern and eastern section of Germany. To be in the center of the territory, the family settled in Berlin. They took an apartment on the elegant Kurfürstendam.

**Diorama of Diesel's workship at the
Maschinenfabrik Augsburg, 1893**

Courtesy Deutsches Museum, Munich

Although selling the Linde ice machines quite successfully, Diesel returned to the idea of his ammonia engine. As fuel ammonia was vastly superior to many other elements, but it was potentially dangerous. In the laboratory he maintained there, he became determined to prove that air could be compressed with relative safety and by imposing fuel particles which this compressed air could cause to ignite and thus increase the heat — or power.

When he had developed his theory, Diesel applied for a patent for the process of "developing a combustion power engine." After lengthy and detailed examination, because the process was believed not to be original, the Reichspatentamt on February 28, 1892, issued patent number 67,207 to Rudolf Diesel.

At first the Augsburg machine works turned down the offer to construct an engine as visualized by Diesel, and his wife Martha suggested that he publish the idea. The "Theory and Construction of a Rational Heat Engine to Replace the Steam Engines and the Currently Known Combustion Engines" appeared in January, 1893. In the meantime the director of the Augsburg Machine Works, Heinrich Buz, had decided to undertake the task of creating a workable engine.

The brochure created great interest and considerable controversy. The main features of the Diesel patent were the heating of pure air in a working cylinder to a temperature substantially above that of ignition temperature of the fuel used. It also provided for the introduction of finely atomized fuel into the compressed air which would develop heat by pushing down the confining piston through what Diesel called "isothermal expansion."

Diesel knew quite well that a wide gap existed between the theoretical concept and the workable engine and the fifteen-year period of patent protection might well be used up to accomplish this development work. The company would have to invest a considerable sum of money and should have enough time to recoup its outlay before the patent ran out and others could benefit from his ideas.

Diesel realized that many details needed yet to be worked out and he augmented his original patent thesis appreciably. For this he received patent number 82,168 in November, 1893. With this additional material, he found many worthy advocates for his engine design, including the directors of the important Krupp and of the Sulzer machine factories.

On February 21, 1893, Diesel signed an agreement with the Augsburg factory to build an engine within six months and to test it extensively, giving them the right to sell the engines in practically all of Germany. On April 10, an agreement was made with Krupp to also build and thoroughly test his engine for the sales rights to the remaining portion of the country. Krupp was to pay Diesel 30,000 marks annually and 37.5 percent of the factory price of engines sold. After that amount reached 500,000 marks, the percentage was to go down to 25 percent of the selling price of engines sold by Krupp. The Sulzer Brothers, however, wanted to wait until tests by the other two manufacturers showed conclusively that the new engine was marketable, but offered to pay Diesel an annual fee of 20,000 marks for an option on the Swiss rights. Diesel refused, writing that he had no interest in money, but only in the perfection of the engine. Realizing soon after his refusal, however, that he indeed needed money, he signed a contract with Sulzers on May 16, 1893.

The Krupp and the Augsburg firms decided to combine their efforts in the development work and concentrated the formidable task of building an engine in a special laboratory at the Augsburg factory. Their "pilot" had to be impressively superior to any commercial engine then on the market.

An able engineer of the Augsburg plant, Lucian Vogel, joined the work force as the inventor's aid. He was an energetic and highly dedicated man.

Rudolf Diesel left Berlin in July and wrote to his wife: "I ride to Augsburg for the most important and decisive moment of my life." A letter from her, full of encouraging words, awaited him at the plant.

The ten-foot high, black iron cylinder for the engine had already been erected. Diesel brought a trunk full of diagrams, drawings, and pamphlets. Work began, using a heavy, brown fuel oil at first. It proved almost impossible to ignite the stuff and kerosene and even refined gasoline was tried instead. The main thing was to get the engine to run, then the fuel problem could be attacked and solved. An air compressor had to be installed to fill the supply tank. A Linde ammonia compressor was used.

The A-frame engine had a cylinder of 150 millimeter (5.91 inch) bore and 400 millimeter (15.75 inch) stroke. It operated on the four stroke cycle principle. The upper portion of the cylinder and the cover were of cast steel, but cast iron was used for the cylinder walls. The top of the piston was rounded and the rod was connected to a large flywheel set into a well below the machine.

The oringinal thin bronze piston rings proved impractical and had to be replaced with cast rings without tension, but not before hundreds of tests with all kinds of material and placement designs. The plunger of the fuel pump and needle were first equipped with asbestos, later with leather. Both proved unsuited, but eventually an asbestos material was found satisfactory. The inlet and exhaust valve were combined, but had to be redesigned to operate properly. Fuel injection took place directly from the pressurized line, controlled by a timing cam. A spray nozzle was positioned at the end of the cylinder itself.

The engine operated at 300 revolutions per minute. Compression tests appeared successful only at 18 atmospheres (atü). The diagrams showed a great negative area and substantial power losses. After much experimentation the compression rose to 21 to 22 atmospheres (about 315 pounds per square inch, or psi) and finally to 33 to 34 atmospheres (about 485 psi). Diesel had theorized a figure twice that high, but Vogel counseled to leave well enough alone at that time.

Rudolf Diesel now reviewed stubbornly all data and examined most carefully all parts which affected the compression.

Diligent studies were made of the correct shape, size, and location of the chamber in the cylinder and the devices for atomization of fuel were checked. Hundreds of diagrams were prepared showing the various curves resulting from numberless tests. The compression chamber, located like a convex scoop in the top of the curved piston, covered an enclosure of 255 cubic centimeters (155.55 cubic inches), but closer inspection revealed that small irregularities produced an additional 157 cubic centimeters (95.77 cubic inches) of piston displacement space. This actually represented an increase of more than 60 percent over the original design.

The work crew proceeded to make a first test of the engine using the fuel injector. Using external power to position the piston properly they then sprayed in gasoline vapor. Anxiously, Rudolf Diesel and Lucian Vogel waited to see if the engine would run. Everyone watched apprehensively. Then, to the utter joy of those present, the engine ran. Ignition had been achieved.

The first diagram showed that compression was up to about 80 atmospheres (1,160 psi), and it may well have been much greater. That none would know for certain.

The indicator exploded, shattering glass and metal, and barely missing the heads of the two most deeply involved persons. Luckily, the solidly built engine withstood the high pressure.

When tests were continued the following day, the engine ran with regular rhythm, but occasionally loud explosions interrupted the uniform pulsation. Thick clouds of black smoke shot out of the exhaust and soon the engine was entirely covered with soot.

The first diagrams were disappointing, showing very low work performance, but eventually the capacity increased. The engine developed 2.15 horsepower, not sufficient to sustain its own operation, but much had been learned about it by observation. A detailed report of this thirty-eight day testing period was made. Diesel sent copies to the Krupp and Augsburg factories.

Heinrich Buz wrote on his copy: "The practical application of the process is proven in this imperfect engine." But Diesel realized that still much work had to be done to build a marketable engine. This one did not even produce enough power for itself.

Rudolf Diesel returned to Berlin to redesign his engine. The family moved to a less expensive apartment in the Charlottenburg area, and with his assistant Johannes Nadrowski set to work on a large drawing table in one of the rooms. Diesel also drafted applications for patents in foreign countries. And he became reacquainted with his wife and their three children.

Right after the New Year's celebration, Rudolf Diesel returned to Augsburg. His former benefactor, Professor Barnickel, had married Rudolf's sister Emma after the death of his wife Betty, and now invited the inventor again to stay at their home.

Tests with the second model engine began in January, 1894. The basic design was retained and cylinder dimensions were also the same as before, but the upper cylinder chamber was of an entirely new design. Inlet and exhaust valves were separated and placed differently than before. The needle valve was placed in a removable housing atop the upper cylinder chamber and close to the entrance of the fuel line into the combustion chamber.

The exhaust valve had a smaller valve in its spindle to assist in the action. The inlet valve also served as safety valve and was controlled by a small hand wheel. The timing mechanism of the valves was left as before, consisting of long rods connected to the fuel pump at the base of the machine. The lubrication of the redesigned fuel pump was achieved by a ring which would touch the oil sump at its lowest dead center point. The combustion chamber was now a cup-shaped separate chamber in the cast iron piston and could easily be enlarged or diminished by removable inserts.

Rudolf Diesel made most of the exhaustive tests himself, but he was assisted by Hans Linder, who had worked on refrigeration engines and by the able mechanic Friedrich Schmucker. Both men later became competent Diesel engineers because of this early intimate development work when the engine was nursed from its infancy to maturity.

But before the comprehensive testing began, all engine parts were scrutinized by means of extreme hydrostatic pressures, the cylinder to 200 atmospheres, cylinder head to 110 atmospheres, and the fuel injector to 160 atmospheres.

The engine was again started through an auxiliary engine. Valve springs were tested, adjusted, and proper tolerances noted. All different results of the changing of the fuel injection needle were recorded. The piston was carefully examined and diagrams made of the compression to determine the reasons for the losses. New rings had been designed — the earlier ones were too loose — but now proved so tight that they exerted a breaking effect as shown by heat tests on the cylinder wall.

Many arrangements were tried again, either two or three pairs, with or without springs, and variously placed. An improvement in compression was noted, but it still fell below the expectations of Diesel.

The shape of the piston top was altered greatly. Rings would slip off the cone-shaped head so it was replaced by a flat center top. To stop the leakage under high pressure all likely materials were tried. The pressure of the several fuels tested — air, gasoline, kerosene, or heavy oils — differed greatly and each presented a different problem.

To test the formation of the spray in outside air, the cylinder head was removed at normal operation of the valves with the engine driven by the auxiliary power. At higher pressures the spray pattern appeared satisfactory, but at lower pressures it formed a solid stream and would not vaporize.

Different procedures for the injection of the fuel were tried directly from the pump. And the injection needle was found to operate successfully so that this use would be maintained later on. To meter the fuel admitted, varying lengths of connecting rods were used. The fuel pump metering mechanism problems seemed just insurmountable. Diesel wanted to inject the fuel directly from the line through the timing of the metering needle, but failed in solving that problem and eventually abandoned the idea entirely.

Then, after many frustrating disappointments, especially with the fuel injection systems, the engine ran under its own power for the first time on February 17, 1894. For one whole minute the Diesel engine ran at about eighty-eight revolutions per minute.

When Hans Linder noticed that the belt which connected the flywheel to the auxiliary engine slackened, and then jerked repeatedly, he realized that the new engine actually pulled the starting engine. He lifted his cap in a silent salute. Rudolf Diesel noted the gesture and understood its meaning. He reached out his hand and clasped that of his helper. Neither man spoke a word. It was a historic occasion and words could add absolutely nothing.

Hope soared that day and Diesel wrote to his wife to come to Augsburg and share the happy triumph. Martha came into the laboratory and raising the lever, started the engine. It ran smoothly.

The shares of the Maschinenfabrik Augsburg rose by 30 percent in a month, according to the Munich newspapers and expectations by Heinrich Buz rose to new heights. Diesel traveled to France to see Frédéric Dyckhoff, an earlier acquaintance, to discuss the location of a new factory to build his engines. On the way home he stopped in Ghent to talk business with the Carels Frères factory directors, in Liège with Cockerill, and Mülhausen with other industrialists. The Carels paid him 20,000 francs for the sales rights for Belgium.

In Augsburg, however, further tests proved that the problem of properly controlled combustion had not yet been completely solved. Tests were made again. Shapes and settings of the injection nozzle were tried, but the back pressure still hampered the operation of the fuel injection apparatus. The back pressure and drop valves were rebuilt. Other means of blowing the fuel into the combustion chamber were tried out.

Getting back to the precise conditions of the successful operating of the engine, a thirty-six minute long run was accomplished at wide open throttle. Diagrams were again made, generally showing unstable combustion. The power output was 13.2 horsepower at 300 revolutions per minute, but still severe friction losses were indicated. A change in the timing mechanism corrected the delayed ignition periods.

But the fuel injection problem gave constant trouble. Forced injection of compressed air appeared to be useful. A workable method had to be found and it was decided that the fuel had to be vaporized when injected. Still, the problem was not solved during six months of systematic searching. Eventually a newly built apparatus placed inside the chamber and redesigned cylinder head produced an increase of the compression to 38 atmospheres, or about 54 psi, but occasional heavy knocks persisted. A patented device by von Zettler of Munich was tested, but it left heavy carbon deposits and created short circuiting.

Nearly three months of effort had resulted in failure and great disappointment. Diesel went to Stuttgart to consult with Robert Bosch who built an apparatus which, after testing, also proved useless.

Word came from France that the engine constructed by Dyckhoff worked better than the one built at Augsburg, but Diesel was not able to bring it to Germany. On October 4, 1894, he wrote to his sponsors admitting his failure to solve the ignition problem and suggesting that gas be used as fuel. The directors gave their consent to use expensive illuminating gas instead.

A new engine was built and a gas line connected to it. When a one-stage compressor proved inadequate a multi-stage unit was tried. The blown air went through a safety cylinder and came into contact with the heated fuel in a pineapple-shaped cylinder, then traveled through a long line into the injection nozzle on top of the cylinder of the engine. Good diagrams of compression, admission, and expansion resulted. Compression was sufficient to effect ignition and the electric ignition provided was actually unnecessary.

This engine operated well enough for the needed demonstration before the Austrian patent officials to secure the earlier purely theoretical patent grant.

Back in Augsburg once again a new engine was built. Refined and revised, this model used the same base and gear as the previous one, but the cylinder diameter was doubled. The bore was 220 millimeters (8.66 inches) but the stroke remained 400 millimeters (15.75 inches). The ratio was 1.82 to 1 against the former 2.67 to 1. The injection nozzle was placed in the cylinder head to concentrate the compressed air there. The valves were again combined because of space limitations.

The metering mechanism was located on top, thus eliminating the long rods. A spark plug was installed in the small combustion chamber for experimentation purposes. The needle housing was redesigned. Two passages were provided, one for gas, the other for liquid fuel. The piston was also of a new design.

On March 30, 1895, patent number 86,633 was issued to Diesel for a method of starting the engine. On January 18, 1896, the patent number 90,544 covering correlated phases, was awarded too.

A new assistant, Fritz Reichenbach, joined Diesel when the new tests began on March 26, 1895. They revealed that only 10 percent of work in the combustion chamber was lost now against 28 percent previously and the enormous 60 percent loss on the first engine design. For one month tests were made with kerosene, then gasoline was used, but combustion was not instantaneously achieved. The engine developed 23 horsepower at 200 revolutions per minute and 34 horsepower at 300 revolutions. It represented 58 percent mechanical efficiency.

On May 1 the anticipated performance was realized. It had taken about two years of strenuous work.

Diesel then devised a friction brake and a new mechanism to atomize the fuel was designed. Several different jets were tried. A double star jet proved satisfactory. Brake tests in June showed 30.8 percent internal thermal efficiency, 54 percent mechanical efficiency, and 16.6 percent brake thermal efficiency. The low mechanical efficiency achieved caused a close examination of all mechanical parts. Better lubrication of piston and rings increased the rating. It rose to 67.2 percent and productive efficiency to 20.26 percent. Greater care in the construction of the engine parts was indicated.

At about that time Wilhelm Hartmann had tested a kerosene engine of his design and Diesel compared the figures in letters to Krupp and Augsburg. Diesel's engine, 58 percent as large as Hartmann's, used only 60 percent of the fuel as his competitor's but produced the same amount of power, although it operated at about 75 percent of its rated capacity.

Still, there was some work to do yet before actual series production could begin, Diesel realized well enough.

Work on the building of a perfect air pump and more accurate gauges was begun. Further tests over long periods provided some pertinent information on engine behavior. For instance, the star jet lasted for only fifty hours of continuous operation.

The chemical engineer Hartenstein from Krupp made a detailed analysis of the exhaust gases and suggested improved utilization of the existing air for better combustion. Greater cooling of the incoming air was essential when the lubricating oil repeatedly caught fire. The bronze piston was replaced by one of harder steel. And some other parts were altered.

A conference of Krupp Werke and Maschinenfabrik Augsburg officials was called on February 20, 1896, to discuss the manufacturing of a marketable Diesel engine. Working drawings were ordered for a one-cylinder engine with a bore of 250 millimeters (9.84 inches) and stroke of 400 millimeters (15.75 inches), a ratio of 1.6 to 1. Immanuel Lauster was one of the young engineers to aid in that work. The drawings were delivered to the factories on April 30, 1896. Friedrich

Schmucker supervised exhaustive testing of the basic production model, which performed well with illuminating gas or kerosene as fuel.

Component parts for the engine were ready for testing. Cylinder, cylinder heads, and cooling jacket were manufactured of cast iron. The smooth combustion chamber was in one unit, between piston and cylinder head without side chamber or bulges. The piston was hollow and water-cooled. Four expander rings were used. The valves were separated. The air and fuel nozzles entered the injector through the side of the cylinder head. The timing mechanism was placed on top and connected with the fuel pump. A housing on the bottom portion of the cylinder contained the valves for the pump. The patent number 95,680 of March 6, 1896, covered these adjustments. As always, safety valves had been placed in all dangerous areas to avoid accidents and during the entire five-year period none of serious nature happened.

Final tests were started on the last day of the year of 1896. Results on January 29, 1897, showed thermal efficiency 31.9 percent and 38.4 per-cent at half load, mechanical efficiency 75.6 percent and 61.5 percent at half load, and productive efficiency 24.2 percent with 23.6 percent at half load. Rudolf Diesel was satisfied with these brake test results.

In July, 1897, the Diesel family moved to Munich. That month, too, the largest and most prestigious gas-engine manufacturing concern, the Deutz Gasmotorenfabrik, signed a contract with the Augsburg-Krupp syndicate for the rights also to build the Diesel engine. Diesel himself received 50,000 marks in cash and 20 to 30 percent of the value of the engines sold. Deutz had seriously questioned the Diesel patents, claiming that their own adviser, Professor Otto Köhler, had published a paper outlining in detail similar ideas later found in the Diesel engine. But this threatened court action never materialized when Diesel stubbornly disregarded the prior claim.

From Krupp, Rudolf Diesel now received annually 50,000 marks and the assurance that this large concern would manufacture the engines. There too, the question of valid patent rights had come up, but with the influence of Heinrich Buz, the Krupp directors had been eventually convinced that they should proceed.

Professor Moritz Schröter was asked to conduct an impartial, exhaustive study of the engine and file an evaluation report. Five years before, the professor had stated publicly his belief in the projected

Courtesy Fried. Krupp Werke

**Munich 1898 Exhibition of diesel engines by
the Krupp, Deutz, and Nürnberg companies**

engine, although based on only theoretical calculations. After completing the testing work, in the detailed findings he now stated that the Diesel engine realized fully all possibilities of the one-cylinder unit and stood easily at the head of all engines then known. Rated 18-20 horsepower at normal speed, fueled with kerosene, the engine converted 26.2 percent of the potential heat energy of the fuel to effective work, far ahead of other engines. Mechanical efficiency was 75 percent at full load and thermal efficiency 34.2 percent at full load and 38.4 percent at half load. The simple method of regulation allowed for a quick change of load conditions, and the elasticity of operation was equal to the steam engine, a definite advantage. The ease of starting a cold engine was not to be overlooked, the professor pointed out, and concluded that it was indeed "the engine of the future."

Representatives from engine manufacturers came to Augsburg from many lands. The Glasgow company, Mirrlees, Watson, and Yargan, eventually acquired the rights for Great Britain. Diesel went to Scotland to sign the contract, after meeting with Lord Kelvin, who advised the Scotsmen that the Diesel patents were valid. The Sulzer Brothers would make and sell the Diesel engines exclusively in Switzerland. In France, Diesel visited with Dyckhoff and inspected the manufacturing facilities at Bar-le-Duc.

Rudolf Diesel also occasionally spoke to several large assemblies about his engine. The high spot of these appearances was the main assembly of the Society of German Engineers at Kassel in 1897. Professor Schröter also made public his report. It was indeed a joyful day for the inventor of the Diesel engine.

From the United States Colonel Edward D. Meier came to inspect the Diesel engine with the engineer Georg Marx of Nürnberg. The wealthy brewery owner Adolphus Busch of St. Louis had sent his personal representative to fully investigate all details of this new engine. The subsequent enthusiastic report made Busch himself hurry to Baden-Baden to deal with Rudolf Diesel. Overwhelmed by the lavish style of the American, Diesel asked boldly for a million marks as fee for the engine rights for the United States. Without hesitation Busch agreed.

In November 1897, the Augsburg factory delivered its first commercial diesel engine, a 76-horsepower unit, to a customer in Kempton.

A new company to manufacture Diesel engines was founded in Augsburg, the Dieselmotorenfabrik, and the organizers paid 100,000 marks to the Augsburg-Krupp syndicate for the rights to build them.

Emmanuel Nobel, the dynamite king, who also owned large oil fields in the Caspian Baku area, met with Diesel in Berlin and in February 1898, founded the Russian Diesel Engine Company of Nürnberg to manufacture engines to be sold in Russia. Diesel received 600,000 marks in cash and 200,000 marks worth of stock in the new corporation.

Diesel then went to England to negotiate with the arms and munitions maker Hiram Maxim. In letters to his wife he complained of severe headaches. Generally, when meetings pressed him or unpleasant news reached him, he suffered these attacks. The reports from the Mirrlees firm of unexpected manufacturing problems did nothing to ease that pain.

Again, a challenger to the patents appeared. Emil Capitaine charged prior rights. The patent office heard the case in April, 1898, then ruled that no infringement could be found. But the angry Capitaine persisted and asked 20,000 marks from Diesel to cease his persecution. Diesel refused, but Capitaine made trouble until his death in 1907.

The Second Power and Works Machine Exhibition opened in Munich in the summer of 1898. Proudly, Rudolf Diesel took his family to the Kollektiv-Ausstellung of the Diesel engines, the first public showing of these new power movers. Four models were shown.

The engines were all A-frame one-cylinder units and were hastily assembled for the showing. A two-cylinder engine, to be exhibited by the Nürnberg company, could not be completed in time. To insure smooth operation, the engines were usually run for a short time before the exhibition opened its gates to the general public.

The Machinenfabrik Augsburg displayed a 30-horsepower engine operating a pump by Brakeman. Fried. Krupp displayed a 35-horsepower machine which turned a high-pressure centrifugal pump by Sulzer. The Maschinenbau A.G. Nürnberg demonstrated a 20-horsepower engine which showed the starting and operating procedure to the visitors. And Deutz exhibited a 20-horsepower engine operating a Linde air liquifying machine.

To properly handle the many complicated foreign and domestic licensing agreements, the Allgemeine Gesellschaft für Dieselmotoren was formed. From this corporation Diesel was to receive 3.5 million marks, but actually got only 1.25 million marks in cash and the balance in stock.

With the engine now in good operating order, Diesel began some extensive tests with various types of fuel. His main purpose earlier had been to build a working machine and the fuel question was deferred. It was not the highest priority. The high viscosity of some oils presented vexing problems, especially the heavy muscut from Baku. Russian solar oils, Galician blue oils, raw naphta, kerosene and petroleum were found suitable as fuel. Experiments were also conducted with pure alcohol, but kerosene was needed for ignition. And much time was expended in tests with coal dust. But the problems of using this relatively inexpensive fuel were just too great to solve and the idea was abandoned.

Considerable effort by Diesel and his engineers was directed toward the perfection of the compound engine. Patented in 1892, this engine consisted of two working cylinders, connected with a larger center cylinder. The working cylinder had a diameter of 200 millimeters (7.87 inches) and the expanison cylinder 510 millimeters (20.08 inches). However, the design proved too complicated and the multitude of problems with this huge machine were too great to solve. Neither Diesel and his aids nor the factory directors were really much interested in further demanding test work.

The Augsburg-Krupp syndicate had spent 443,335.31 marks (over $105,000) on the development work of the Diesel engine over the four year period. Other incidental expenses brought the total to about 600,000 marks.

Diesel received an annual fee of 30,000 marks from the syndicate, but his life style had sky-rocketed and was appallingly expensive. And with it all, the terrible headaches also increased, so that eventually his doctor suggested complete rest. Diesel entered a sanitorium near Munich, but when that period of solitude brought not the expected relief, he went to Meran in the Tyrol for an extended stay. He lived there for two months, hiking and enjoying the magnificent Alpine scenery.

Soon after he returned to Munich in April, the usual hurried conferences, meetings, and dinners again took up most of Diesel's time. He made bad investments and worried over them. Too proud to ask the professional advice of bankers, he often took extremely poor risks. In a petroleum venture he lost about 300,000 marks. The Diesel Engine Company in Augsburg collapsed because of bad management and caused a considerable financial loss to the inventor.

Late in 1898 the Maschinenfabrik Augsburg merged with the Maschinenbaugesellschaft Nürnberg to form M.A.N. (Machine-factory Augsburg-Nürnberg). The first Diesel engines built and sold caused the manufacturers abundant troubles. Often they did not perform as expected and servicing them was made difficult because of the lack of expert mechanics.

It had been hoped that the various license holders would freely exchange their experiences in the construction as well as new ideas for mutual benefit, but this hope was not fulfilled. Diesel traveled about, trying to assist wherever problems existed and encourage the lagging spirits of several manufacturers of his engines.

Despite problems, the Diesels built a palatial home above the Isar River in Munich. For two years this extravagant construction caused anguish and disappointments to the fastidious proprietor. The furnishings were most sumptious, befitting the 700,000 mark mansion, and here again, the decorators and craftsmen took up much time and often got on the nerves of Diesel. No wonder then that after the elegant home was finished, it proved no haven for the harrassed tenant. He went to the Bodensee for a rest. There Diesel met Graf von Zeppelin who was busy with the building of an airship, after retirement from the Army with the rank of general.

Courtesy Sautter, Harlé et Cie

Two-cylinder marine diesel engine by Sautter Harlé & Cie., Paris

In these restful surroundings Diesel found time to assemble the notes for a treatise on the social philosophy he had espoused over the years and to publish them. He believed in ways of freeing the workers from enslavement, to be brought about by the utilization of his engines. He saw interdependence, a solidarity of interests between the owner class and the working class, rather than the conflict which presently existed. It was, to him, unnatural, unjust, and unendurable. The remedy was for every worker to save one penny a day so that he could buy at least one share in his employing company.

A two-volume work, called "Solidarismus" was finally printed in 1903, but it was not accepted by the general public and was quickly forgotten.

Rudolf Diesel went to Paris to attend the 1900 International Exhibition and to see the five Diesel engines exhibited there. Four of them were built by the Bar-le-Duc factory. They were awarded the Grand Prix of the fair.

By 1901, a total of thirty-one companies were licensed to build and sell Diesel engines in eleven countries of the world. A survey showed in 1902 that 359 Diesel engines were in use, developing an aggregate 12,367 horsepower. The following year, the total engines in use were 463.

Some of these installations created controversies. In Budapest, for instance, the largest consumer of the municipal electricity acquired a Diesel engine to generate his own power more economically. When the power company then lost its best customer and the general rates went up to compensate for that loss of revenue, the infuriated people blamed the Diesel engine for the increase, and organized a demonstration against it. But elsewhere installations were usually more peacefully accepted.

In Denmark, the Burmeister and Wain of Copenhagen, who had signed an agreement with Diesel in 1897, did not build engines until 1903, based on the Augsburg design. In 1904, they constructed ten engines ranging in output from 8 to 160 horsepower. Two four-stroke eight-cylinder direct reversible marine engines of 1,250 horsepower each were built for the *Selandia* a 4,950-ton cargo vessel of the East Asiatic Company. The ship also used two auxiliary Diesel engines of 250 horsepower each. An average cruising speed of eleven knots could be maintained on her successful, 22,000 mile maiden voyage early in 1912. This proved beyond doubt the usefulness, economy and reliability of Diesel engines for ocean vessels.

Courtesy M.A.N.

**First large installation of six MAN diesel units
at Kiev, Russia, 1903-1904**

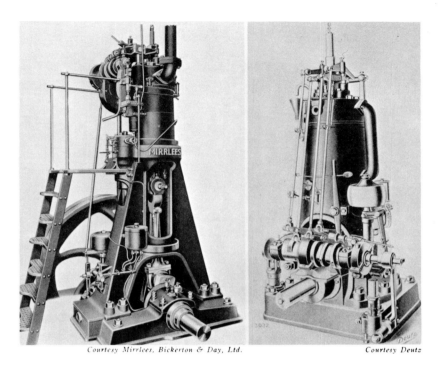

Courtesy Mirrlees, Bickerton & Day, Ltd.   Courtesy Deutz

**First Mirrlees diesel engine of 1897 in Britain
and the 1900 engine built by Deutz**

When in early 1903 a Paris canal barge was powered by a Diesel engine the inventor himself rode in this unique conveyance. His engines were successfully utilized as a maritime power unit now in addition to their more general stationary utilitarian purposes. The firm Anciens Établissement Sautter-Harlé, specializing in marine engines, began in 1903 to develop a reversible Diesel engine. They built a horizontal opposed piston unit of 120 horsepower at 400 revolutions per minute and installed two such engines in the pioneer submarine Z. By 1904 Sautter-Harlé built four-cylinder, four-stroke Diesel engines of 300 horsepower at 340 revolutions per mintue for other submarines and by 1907 six-cylinder engines of 700 horsepower were produced.

In Sweden the Diesel engines were built by the Aktiebolag Diesels-Motorer, founded by M. Wallenberg and O. Lamm, the license holders. Already in July, 1898, the first 20-horsepower engine was delivered to the State Railways. By 1901, the engineers had reduced the weight of the one-cylinder unit by half and the fuel consumption of 193 grams per horsepower remained a record low for years. When K. J. Hesselman designed a simplified two-stroke direct reversible marine engine, installations in sea going vessels quickly followed. By 1907 the first Diesel-engined motorship crossed the Atlantic. And in 1911 a 180-horsepower Diesel engine carried Roald Amundsen to the pole.

Mirrlees, who had built a 50-horsepower Diesel engine in 1898, delivered, after a slow start, in 1903 two three-cylinder and one four-cylinder units as auxiliary power plants for the battleship Dreadnaught. By 1906, lighter weight four-cylinder marine engines of 120-horsepower were built for subsidiary naval craft.

The Sulzer Brothers had built their first Diesel engine in May, 1898.

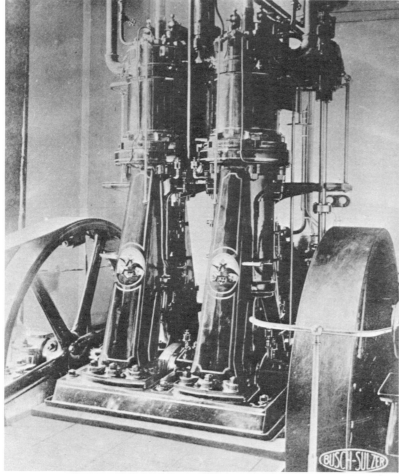

Courtesy Busch-Sulzer

First diesel engine built in the United States by Sulzer in Anheuser-Busch brewery, 1898

When the London Diesel Engine Company placed an order for twelve Diesel units of 35-horsepower each, serious manufacture was begun at Winterthur. A standard four-stroke Diesel engine of 40 horsepower per cylinder was developed and manufactured in units of 1, 2, and 3 cylinders. More than 40 years later an engine delivered in 1904 to Port Said, Egypt, was still in operation.

In Russia, the Nobel factory at St. Petersburg had built its first Diesel engines in 1899 and the following year constructed three units of about 100 horsepower each to be used in their Baku oil fields. Nobel licensed the Kolomna Machine Factory in 1902 to build the engines and that company constructed fifty-two units of 150 horespower each to power pipelines from Baku to Batum. In 1903 the Nobel-owned steamer *Wandal* was equipped with three three-cylinder four-stroke Diesel engines of Stockholm manufacture. Fuel costs of the vessel, plying the Volga River and the Caspian Sea were only 20 percent of those of a steam powered vessel. In 1904 the oil tanker *Ssarmat* of the Nobel fleet was Diesel-powered, the first such carrier of many, by engines made in St. Petersburg.

The Sulzers suplied marine engines for freight and passenger lake vessels in Switzerland.

In Italy, Franco Tosi of Legnano, acquired a license to build Diesel engines in 1903, but the company needed four years to complete its first engine.

In 1905 the Carels Brothers exhibited at the Lìege Fair a 500-horsepower marine Diesel engine, then the largest built. But three years before that, in 1902, the M.A.N. sold a Diesel engine to the city government in Kiev for generating electricity. An order for four more units with a total output of 1,600 horsepower followed quickly, and two more such units were added forthwith.

As he had in every industrialized country, Diesel had also applied for a patent in the United States, but it was not until three years later that he received on July 16, 1895, patent number 542,846 for his engine. The Canadian patent was issued to him in November, 1893.

The Diesel Motor Company of America was founded by Busch in 1898, but no actual manufacture of engines was planned. Two Diesel engines were ordered from the Nürnberg and the Deutz factories. The Nürnberg engine arrived in New York in March and the Deutz engine in July of 1898. Anton Böttcher came to install them in a laboratory near the office of the company, rigged with a 15-kilowatt direct-current dynamo. On April 23, 1898, a Diesel engine ran for the first time in the United States. On May 7, it was exhibited at the Electrical Exposition at Madison Square Garden in New York. The company had paid the Nürnberg factory $3,300 for the 20-horsepower engine and sold it to the Morgan Construction Company for $1,800. In 1899, Seib Brothers Woodworking Company of New Jersey paid $2,400 for the other engine.

Late in 1900 Adolphus Busch told the directors of the company that over a hundred thousand dollars had been spent to develop a market for the Diesel engines, but that no tangible results had been achieved. The first engine built by them had cost $7,955, but was sold to the brewing plant of Anheuser Busch for $3,223. It was decided to sell the remaining shares of stock, worth then $286,000 and build a factory to produce the engines themselves. However, when the International Power Company of New Jersey agreed to invest $250,000 to form the American Diesel Engine Company, engines were to be built under the guidance of that experienced firm. The first, American made, Diesel engine was a three-cylinder unit of 75-horsepower and was tested in April, 1902. By midyear of 1903 a total of 27 Diesel engines were in use in the United States and 66 units were under construction. The ailing company seemed on the way to recovery.

In June, 1904, Rudolf Diesel boarded the *Pretoria* at Kiel for a trip to the United States. The *Morning World* of New York listed him in the published passenger list as Dr. R. Diesel, the noted inventor from Munich. After two days at the Waldorf hotel, he took a train to St. Louis, where he was a guest of the Busch home. Diesel visited the World's Fair, the Louisiana Purchase Exposition, but disappointedly noted that only very few technical and scientific exhibits were shown. He went to Denver by train, then hired a car to see the Pikes Peak and Garden of the Gods areas. In San Francisco the melting pot of Oriental and Occidental people made quite an impression on the sensitive German visitor. Returning east, he stopped at Salt Lake City and liked the most remarkable settlement.

But Diesel was disappointed in the rather unimpressive activities of the American Diesel company and pondered the promising future of his engine in this fabulously rich and extensive country.

Only a year later, in 1905, the Power and Machine Company of Cudahy, Wisconsin, began the manufacture of Diesel engines, but

Courtesy Busch-Sulzer

Three-cylinder diesel engine built by American Diesel Engine Co., 1907

business of the American Diesel Engine Company never became profitable. In 1908, Busch acquired all assets of the corporation and let the venture fade out. In 1911, Busch made another effort and founded the Busch-Sulzer Brothers Diesel Engine Company. A new plant was built in St. Louis where the Sulzer K series of four-stroke single action engines were to be built in four cylinder sizes with bore of from 10.5 inches to 19 inches, and with an output of 120 to 520 horsepower. Their manufacture continued actually until 1920.

In 1910 the Otto Engine Company, licensed by Deutz, began the construction of Diesel engines in Philadelphia. The New London Ship and Engine company built Diesel engines for the United States Navy.

One of their first installations, two years later, was a 300-horsepower unit for an oil barge, and four years later a 2,400-horsepower unit for the *Maumee*.

The Fulton Iron Works of St. Louis built Diesel engines of the Franco Tosi design. When the Worthington Pump and Machinery Corporation took over the Cudahy firm, production was concentrated in a one-cylinder horizontal, four-stroke with air injection engine. Later, marine engines were also built by that firm. And in 1912 Allis Chalmers of Milwaukee and Fairbanks, Morse and Company of Beloit, Wisconsin, began Diesel engine construction. The former built horizontal, four-stroke with air injection engines up to six cylinders, while the latter manufactured a series of vertical engines in two cylinder sizes in units of 1, 2, 3, 4, and 6 cylinders. By the time of Rudolf Diesel's death, the United States Diesel engine industry was well on its way to take its place with that in other countries.

Back home in Munich, after his American trip, Rudolf Diesel had to face his rapidly deteriorating financial situation. His living expenses were exceedingly high and his investments excessively poor. He had lost heavily on oil speculations in Galicia. The real estate investments of about a million marks, much of a highly speculative nature, did not produce income but had even appreciably deteriorated instead. Shares in the Allgemeine Gesellschaft never paid any dividends either. And the company formed to produce Diesel engines quickly while the established manufacturing firms appeared too slow to exploit the machines, finally collapsed, but not after Diesel himself had added huge sums to avert this disaster which might possibly in the minds of the public discredit his engines. The unproductive and dormant corporation was not liquidated until 1911.

It was estimated that by 1905 Rudolf Diesel had lost some three to three and a half million marks.

Well accustomed now to the life style of a man with unlimited funds, Diesel found it almost impossible to cut down on his own living expenses, and neither did the family members stint on much of anything. However, the upstairs rooms of their home were changed into working offices. On a large drawing table, Heinrich Deschamp helped design a small Diesel engine, believed to be suitable for street vehicles, and this model, exhibited at the Brussel's Fair in 1910, received the Grand Prix. But the 5-horsepower engine did not prevail. Neither was a four-cylinder engine practical for such purposes, although Diesel held out high hopes

Six-cylinder submarine diesel engine built by Krupp in 1913

for that creation. It was not until much more had been learned about the engines that a suitable type for vehicles was developed.

In the summer of 1907 the Diesel family went to France for a vacation. They were packed into the large, open red touring NAG automobile with Papa Diesel as chauffeur. They spent a week in the Loire river region and visited Blois, the birthplace of Denis Papin, who had given the world the steam engine in 1690. It was a pilgrimage for Diesel who admired the French scientist deeply, explaining that he too was "born too early for his work." Later, in Paris, the family visited the old museum where a statue of Papin stood in the entrance yard. Diesel stood there in silent homage, deep in thought. Then they returned to Munich.

There were again many trips on business, to Vienna, to St. Petersburg, and plans for another visit to St. Louis in 1912 were completed. Before that, however, Diesel was invited to be a judge at the world's fair at Turin and to attend the World Congress of Mechanical Engineers in London. He sat on the dias with Sir Charles Parsons who in 1884 had invented the steam turbine. Diesel made an enthusiastically received speech in English.

The trip to the United States was mainly for council with the American company, and to create publicity and prestige for the Diesel engines. The maiden voyage of the luxury liner *Titanic* would come too late for the Diesels, and they had to take another ship which would land them in New York in March rather than mid-April. That was the date for the ground breaking ceremonies in St. Louis for a new Diesel engine manufacturing plant.

Upon their arrival in New York, newspaper reporters interviewed them and Diesel found himself mentioned prominently in the daily press. Even the heavy Sunday editions carried detailed descriptions of his engines, as did the New York American on April 14, 1912, "Dr. Diesel Explains his Economical Crude Oil Engine." The article was authoritatively written and placed undoubtedly by the public relations staff for the American Diesel Engine Company.

Diesel spoke to various assemblies during this visit with addresses at the United States Naval Academy, Cornell University, and the convention of the American Society of Mechanical Engineers at Cooper Union in New York being the most important. There he emphasized the success of the Diesel engine as a prime mover and pointed out the many important installations of stationary units to generate electric power as well as the vast use in the maritime field. But the expectation of widest use in the vast network of railroads seemed to receive the greatest emphasis of the speaker.

The Mirrlees Company was then making the first Diesel electric installation in big ships. One of the innovations was the development of an engine quite suitable to power a battle tank, and another to adopt the Diesel engine to operate on up to 90% coal-tar oil.

Also by 1912 Tosi had launched into design and construction of huge power plants. A 2,400-horsepower unit was soon to be the most powerful Diesel engine in the world.

Already in 1910 Sulzer had built a single cylinder engine with a 1,000 millimeter (39.37 inch) bore which developed 2,000 horse-power at 150 revolutions per minute. The following year an even larger four-cylinder engine was started with each cylinder developing 850 horse-power.

But Diesel noted that for railroad use, tests were rather inconclusive and even frustrating. It was not until 1914 that the Prussian and the Saxon Railways used Diesel engines. By then, five years had been spent and over two million marks on testing.

By 1912 Diesel engines were powering 365 ships, including at least 60 merchant vessels. The list included the submarine fleet of France, then the largest of any nation. Even the largest sailing ship, the *La France* with 70,000 square feet of sail aloft, had two 1,800 horse-power Diesel engines below.

At the time Diesel attended the ground breaking ceremonies of the new manufacturing facilities in St. Louis, he reflected on the sad fact that only about ten Diesel engines were then in use in the United States. Out of a total of over 70,000 units then operating in the world, it was a dismal number indeed.

After the auspicious Cooper Union address, Diesel met with Thomas Edison at the modest cottage which also served as laboratory of the famous inventor. The 65-year old Edison's repeated assertion that a successful inventor is primarily a superb coordinator of the works of other inventors did not impress Diesel at all. But it was certainly a fact that Edison had been most successful in correlating the work of his many assistants who generally collectively solved the problems given them.

Returning home from the United States, Rudolf Diesel also returned to the worsening realities of his tragic financial problems. His real estate speculations had cost him a total of 600,000 marks. He was forced to mortgage his house and discharge most of the servants. By the middle of 1912 Diesel's financial failures had amounted to nearly ten million marks.

Understandably his headaches returned to torment him and the painful gout remained chronic. He hoped that his book on "The Origin of the Diesel Engine" would bring him some monetary returns when it would be published by the prestigious Julius Fischer Verlag at the end of the year. He had worked on this comprehensive, scholarly history for some time, but it was put in final form only after he incorporated portions of a lecture he had given before the Shipbuilding Technical Union in Berlin.

Diesel now traveled again to visit and to talk business in Paris, London, Amsterdam, and other places where Diesel engines were manufactured. Early in 1913 he and Martha went to Sicily for a short vacation, and stopped briefly at Capri, Naples, and Rome. Alone he visited the Bavarian Alps and climbed again the Sauling and saw the Sulzers at Winterthur. He spent some time at the International Builders Exhibition in Leipzig and flew in Zeppelin's airship *Sachsen*, although previously he had considered it too dangerous. That airship had been on regular scheduled flights between German cities that year and had a perfect safety record.

That summer, at their home, the Diesels also entertained Colonel Meier from St. Louis, George Carels of Ghent, and Sir Charles Parsons of Britain, among other prominent and dear friends.

Still, the huge debts caused Rudolf Diesel not only terrific headaches but also extreme melancholy and despondency, although he felt that much of that condition was hereditary.

To lift his spirits, an invitation came from England for Diesel to come for the ground breaking ceremonies for a new Diesel engine plant at Ipswich, where he would also be a consultant at 1,000 pounds annually. And Carels asked him to visit before at Ghent. Both men planned to go to England together, and Carels had arranged for his good friend to speak in London at a Royal Automobile Club meeting on November 30. The engineer Alfred Laukman would accompany them.

A week before the trip, Martha left to visit relatives at Remscheid. He gave the servants a long weekend off and spent the few days alone with his son Rudolf, showing him where valuable papers were kept and when the servants returned, they noted that a considerable quantity of paper had been burned in the fireplace.

In Frankfurt Rudolf Diesel spent two weeks with his daughter Hedy and son-in-law Arnold von Schmidt and visited the Adler Werke where he was a director. Martha joined them then for a short stay. As a going-away present Diesel bought an expensive overnight travel case for Martha which she was not to open until the following week.

Diesel took a train for Ghent, stopping at the then quite elegant Hotel de la Poste on the Place d'Armes. From there he wrote a letter to Martha, a rather strange, confused, and poetic one in German and French. He addressed it to Frankfurt, but used the Munich street address, in error or confusion.

On the afternoon of November 29 the three men, Diesel, Carels and Laukman, boarded the channel steamer *Dresden* at Antwerp for the night crossing to Harwich.

They dined and enjoyed pleasant conversation. Diesel was in good spirits, Carels noted, but hardly touched his wine. After dinner, they walked around the promenade deck and after leaving the river and entering the channel waters they decided to retire to their respective cabins. They had left a call for six-fifteen.

When Diesel did not appear for breakfast the next morning, Carels went to his stateroom. His bunk had not been slept in, but his watch was placed on the bedside table with his notebook. The key was in the suitcase. Carels reported Diesel missing to the captain, but nothing had been noticed by the watchman on duty during the night. A thorough search yielded no trace of the missing passenger, whose neatly folded coat was found on the afterdeck.

Ten days later, the Belgian pilot steamer *Coertsen* picked up a floating body and after removing some items for identification returned it to the sea in the accustomed manner. At Vlissingen, Eugen Diesel identified the coin purse, medicine container, and spectacle case as that of his father.

*   *   *   *   *

On a mild evening in late September my wife Betty and I boarded a freighter at Antwerp for our journey home to California, via London. Schedules are notoriously uncertain because the business of freighters is cargo and not passengers. The ship sailed that evening. The huge, two-stroke cycle Diesel engines chugged in a heavy rhythm and we moved slowly down the Schelde River. When we reached the pilot station at Vlissingen we came to a stop to let the pilot off. Then the engines again took up their familiar thumping beat, accelerating gradually to the cruising speed of the vessel. Night had fallen. We stood at the railing, deep in contemplation, looking into the dark waters. We had just spent over six months in Europe, researching libraries and museums and visiting factories and many cities where the subject of our biography had lived and worked and vacationed. Now we were anxious to get back to Santa Barbara.

It was exactly fifty years to the day when Rudolf Diesel had taken the same route and was at the same spot at the same time — from which he never returned.

Early Vehicular Diesel Engines

Rudolf Diesel had written about his experimental work at the Maschinenfabrik Augsburg that on February 17, 1894, "we finally achieved the first free running at 88 revolutions per minute for about one minute duration, but had to turn off almost at once because the exhaust valve stuck suddenly."

This first real success with the new engine was only possible after several changes had been made in the basic idea Diesel had conceived in 1892. The more important changes were the *Einblasung* (blowing-in) of the fuel instead of the not yet successfully mastered injection of it, and the lowering of the compression ratio from the projected 250 atmospheres (3,670 pounds per square inch) to 30 atmospheres (440 pounds per square inch). To achieve a continuously steady power output actually another three years of greatly frustrating and terribly demanding testing work were required from the time of the first running of the diesel engine. And one of the most important problems to solve was the regular and uniform injection of the fuel, but when eventually compressed air was forced into an atomizer, where the fuel was mixed with this compressed air and forced into the cylinder, success was assured.

Exactly three years after the first successful running of the diesel engine, on February 17, 1897, the first performance tests were made by Moritz Schröter, professor of *Mechanischer Wärmelehre* (mechanical heat studies) at the Technical University at Munich. He observed an output of 17.8 horsepower at 154 revolutions per minute and a fuel consumption rate of 238 grams per horsepower, equaling a heat utilization *(Wärmeausnützung)* of 26 percent. That achievement exceeded the productivity which had been measured up to then in gas or oil engines, and presaged a tremendous future for the diesel engine.

Rudolf Diesel spoke of the development work of his engine to the assembled members of the German Society of Engineers at their annual convention in Kassel on June 16, 1897, and Schröter gave the results of his efficiency tests, concluding "that this engine should be considered a starting point of an industry now reaching ultimate development." After overcoming several vexing problems and some significant construction changes the engine was rapidly developed as stationary power unit for generators and marine vessels, but for the use in railroad locomotives the comprehensive tests made were rather discouraging.

When Jacob Lohner, owner of the Wiener Hofwagenfabrik, intended to build automotive vehicles, Diesel wrote to him on September 4, 1897, that "special peculiarities of my engine will almost certainly show it to be superior to all others." However, soon after that, Diesel had to retreat from his quick certainty and was forced to caution against early hopes for success. When the engine building entered the critical period of 1898 to 1900, all plans for adaption to automotive vehicles were quietly shelved.

When in 1907 the original patent of Rudolf Diesel, Number 67207 of 1892, ran out, several unlicensed companies began the manufacture of diesel engines. Nearly all of these large stationary engine manufacturers recognized the fact that the new type engine had become a most serious competitor to the types they now produced.

At the Benz & Cie., Rheinische Gasmotoren Fabrik, the diesel engine was considered a powerful rival to their gas engines, which while actually then more economical to operate were more expensive to maintain. They were also slow in achieving their power output while the diesel engines supplied power right at the start. The Benz directors decided to enter into the manufacture of diesel engines at once.

**Chief Engineer
Prosper L'Orange**

Prosper L'Orange, the auspicous test engineer of the Gasmotoren Fabrik Deutz near Cologne, was engaged early in 1909 by Benz to direct that new development work at their Mannheim factory. Deutz had begun in July 1897 to build its first 20-horsepower diesel engine, a stationary A-frame type. It was one of the first operational diesel engines and was exhibited at the Second Power and Works Machine Exhibition in Munich in 1898 along with the products of three other diesel engine builders.

At that time two different systems were being explored by the test engineers to make the diesel engine operate satisfactorily under all adverse conditions. The construction of the engines of the orthodox design was with fuel injection by means of compressed air *(Druckluft-Einblasung)* which resulted in a cylinder output of from 25 to 60 horsepower at about 200 revolutions per minute. The other was the construction of lighter engines without this supercharged air but with a fuel-air injection *(Einspritzung)* system and with an engine speed of about 400 revolutions per minute, and suitable for transportable engine units. For this approach to the problem, taken by Prosper L'Orange, he developed a pre-combustion chamber system for which the Benz & Cie. received the patent Number 230,517 Klasse 46a, Gruppe 2, from the Kaiserliche Patentamt on March 14, 1909.

According to this patent a separate chamber located in the cylinder head and called the *Vorkammer* (pre-chamber) was to be connected with the working cylinder by means of a small opening. The fuel was to be injected into this pre-chamber, atomized in it, and the highly compressed air causing self-ignition would partly burn it. The pressure thus achieved would then atomize the rest of the fuel and force it into the working cylinder. In order to complete this process in an engine of conventional design, an especially large and rather costly supercharging system was needed.

However, in these early tests L'Orange and his assistants ran into many difficulties. The main problem confronting them was with the open nozzle which had also caused Rudolf Diesel untold troubles. Drops of fuel would cling to it at the end of the injection period and the resulting deposit would block the nozzle again and again, making a continuous operation of the engine impossible. It was just impossible to construct at that time the necessary highly sophisticated suitable injection equipment which would supply exactly the correct amount of fuel to each cylinder and so eliminate the possibility of any combustion deposits.

Diesel also made an effort to build an engine suitable for vehicles together with Heinrich Dechamps of Brussels, who enjoyed a good reputation for building motorized carriages. Dechamps intended to construct a diesel-type engine based on the four-cylinder 42 horsepower gasoline engine of Saurer manufacture. It was to develop 30 horsepower at 800 revolutions per minute.

Development work was undertaken at the newly founded Safir Company at Zurich. But the progress proved disappointingly slow. The selected four-piston fuel pump did not achieve the necessary precision for measuring the fuel nor regulating the correct amount needed at the various loads. The Safir Company experienced finanical difficulties and further development work was moved to the A.G.St. Georgen at Zurich. This also ceased eventually. The general feeling then was that the time for development was too short, but the lack of a dependable injection and regulation apparatus was the decided reason for this early failure.

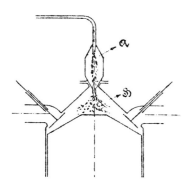

Patent document for pre-combustion chamber design of 1909, with drawings

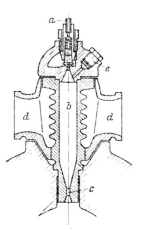

KAISERLICHES PATENTAMT.

PATENTSCHRIFT

— № 230517

KLASSE **46** *a.* GRUPPE 2.

BENZ & CIE, RHEINISCHE GASMOTORENFABRIK AKT.-GES. IN MANNHEIM.

Verbrennungskraftmaschine für flüssige Brennstoffe.

Patentiert im Deutschen Reiche vom 14. März 1909 ab.

Bei den nach dem Gleichdruckverfahren arbeitenden Verbrennungskraftmaschinen ist zum Einblasen des Brennstoffes Preßluft erforderlich.

Statt der Preßluft können zum Zerstäuben auch gespannte Verbrennungsgase, welche, wie z. B. bei Haselwanders Methode, durch die Vorexplosion eines Hilfsgemisches erzeugt werden, verwendet werden.

Eine solche Vorexplosion bringt jedoch stets Unregelmäßigkeiten und Zufälligkeiten in den Arbeitsvorgang hinein, da sie bald zu früh, bald zu spät, bald zu heftig und bald zu schwach ist.

Bei der Erfindung ist deshalb solch eine Vorexplosion vermieden, und der Überdruck zum Zerstäuben in den Arbeitsraum hineintretenden Brennstoffes wird dadurch erzeugt, daß derselbe durch eine Erweiterung der Einspritzdüse (Kammer) hindurchgespritzt wird. In dieser werden Teile von ihm während der ganzen Dauer des Durchtrittes teils vollkommen verbrennen, teils sich zersetzen, teils nur verdampfen.

Durch diese drei Vorgänge: Verbrennung, Zersetzung und Verdampfung wird bei richtiger Regulierung während der ganzen Durchtrittsdauer des Brennstoffes eine Volumenvergrößerung des Inhaltes von *A* und bei entsprechender Bemessung des Inhaltes der Kammer, der Zwischenöffnung und der Einspritzmenge pro Zeiteinheit ein stetiges Überströmen von Gasen mit dem Brennstoff zugleich stattfinden.

Die sofortige Entzündung des durch die Kammer in den Zylinder strömenden Brennstoffes wird hierbei durch entsprechend hohe Kompression, eventuell Beheizung der Kammer durch äußere Flamme (besonders beim Anlassen), sowie durch die nicht abgeführte Wärme der ungekühlten Wandungen gesichert.

PATENT-ANSPRUCH:

Verbrennungskraftmaschine für flüssige Brennstoffe, bei welcher der Brennstoff sofort beim Eintritt in die Maschine verbrennt, dadurch gekennzeichnet, daß der flüssige Brennstoff durch eine heiße Kammer gespritzt wird, wobei er teilweise vollkommen verbrennt, teilweise sich zersetzt und teilweise verdampft und durch diese Umsetzungen auf dem Wege durch die Kammer den Druck in derselben über den Druck im Arbeitsraume des Zylinders erhöht, wodurch mit dem Brennstoff zugleich während der ganzen Durchtrittsdauer Gase und Dämpfe in den Zylinder strömen und dabei den Brennstoff zerstäuben.

Hierzu 1 Blatt Zeichnungen.

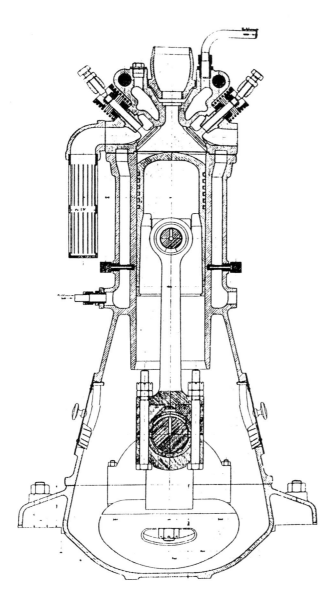

Drawing of the 1909 Benz test engine

Eventually the test engineers were able to reach a continuous running of their test engine for eight days and nights. Fuel consumption was about 245 grams per horsepower. Close examination showed that pistons and chamber were covered only slightly with soot, but the nozzle was still heavily coated with it. Despite all diligent endeavors by all persons involved and using every possible device, the problem proved insurmountable and it was not possible to develop the diesel engine to the point of marketing. Consequently the interest of the Benz directors in the entire diesel engine project declined immensely.

To add to the difficulties encountered in the testing of the new engine was the fact that all of the manufacturing facilities for automobile construction were moved into a new plant in Mannheim-Waldhof, and the chief engineer L'Orange, while working on the diesel engine project, also had to design new types of stationary engines to be built in this factory then employing the most modern manufacturing methods. The new line was a series of P engines of 2, 4, 6, and 8 horsepower. They used petroleum as starting fuel and after a warm-up period operated satisfactorily with napthaline. They were most durable and in fact were widely used in Russia. These newly designed engines did indeed put new life into the stationary engine department of the Benz company and sales increased appreciably over those of the past years.

For large power units a simplified diesel engine was constructed in the usual upright-A style, utilizing a two-stage air compression system. To supply the demand for a marine engine, Benz in the spring of 1910, upon the suggestion of L'Orange, acquired a license from the Swedish engineer Knut Jonas Hesselman. He had the rights to a two-stroke diesel engine which utilized the circulating pumps also for the reversing of the engine. The construction of the seals and atomizer were also unique. In fact, such a Hesselman engine had been used by Roald Amundsen successfully on the polar expedition on his *Fram*. The Benz company delivered several of such engines until the outbreak of World War I.

All further development work on the diesel engine with the patented pre-chamber combustion system ceased. It had not been a success. The efforts of the entire engineering staff were now concentrated on submarine power units instead.

However, Rudolf Diesel expected a great future for a vehicle engine and on September 15, 1913, he made drawings which suggested to him that "the vehicle engine failed because of the undependable injection pump and the inability to adjust the injection pump to the varying demands of the engine." He also wrote, "I still hold the definite belief that the automobile engine will come and then I consider my task as finished."

Still for several years Hesselman and L'Orange exchanged ideas on developing the Diesel engine with special emphasis on the vexing problem of direct fuel injection. When in 1917 the Swedish engineer wrote that he would soon test a new method of injection, L'Orange advised against it, "you will get into the land of unlimited disappointments with that," because he was then terribly disappointed not having been able to solve that problem himself. He had about given up on that project.

However, that same year an engineer at the Ljusne-Woxna-Works in Sweden, Harry Leissner, had successfully developed a pre-chamber system engine and thus solved the problem of injection. He received the German patent Number 302,239 in 1917. That engine was called the Ellwe-engine.

But it was not until the end of the war in 1918 when L'Orange heard of the Leissner solution. The Benz company then purchased such an engine and L'Orange examined it very closely. Actually their own pre-combustion chamber patent had expired because the added fees for an extension had not been paid, but luckily the war had automatically extended the usual period. Examination proved that the Leissner solution came under the Benz patent.

The Ellwe engine had three particular features. Firstly, it had a punctured tube that encompassed the stream of the sprayed fuel and was somewhat similar to the uncooled, long pre-chamber of the L'Orange design. Secondly, it used an enclosed injection nozzle, designed by McKechnie, who had developed this system for the diesel engines with fuel injection for the British submarine service. This injection nozzle had on the end a punctured valve stem, which was closed by means of a valve needle under spring pressure. When the pressure in the fuel line reached a specific point, the needle opened so that the atomization of the fuel remained steady at all loads and revolutions of the engine. And thirdly, there was a stem hollowed at the end which reached into the cylinder chamber. To start the cold engine, this stem would be removed by turning it like a screw and in its hole would be placed a roll of blotting paper, drenched with salpeter (potassium nitrate). This paper would be ignited to start the engine and placed

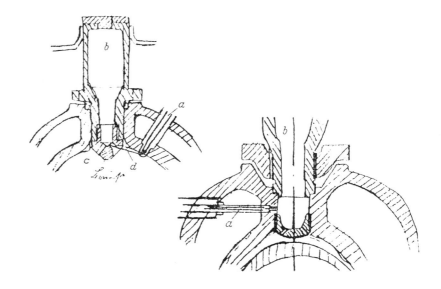

Sketch of pre-combustion chamber by L'Orange, 1910

burning into the pre-chamber so that it caused the initial firing and started the turning of the engine. It was an effective but rather awkward method.

Break tests with the Leissner Ellwe-engine showed good burning of fuel at constant revolutions and under all loads. But it developed that eventually the free end of the nozzle burned up. Still, when the engine was kept running even without the free end, it operated satisfactorily under that condition.

Although all development work on the pre-chamber diesel engine had, of course, completely ceased during the war years at the Mannheim works, now partly because of the encouragement supplied by the nicely operating diesel engine and partly because of the serious economic conditions in the country resulting from the devastating war, interest in this fuel saving engine was intensified. The activity in the developing work was accelerated immensely. Working with L'Orange, the test engineer Ludwig Gentzen and the head of the patent bureau Otto Malms were able to file for a new patent on the Combustion Engine

DEUTSCHES REICH

AUSGEGEBEN
AM 17. JUNI 1924

REICHSPATENTAMT

PATENTSCHRIFT

№ 397142

KLASSE **46a** GRUPPE 2

(B 88823 I/46a)

Benz & Cie., Rheinische Automobil- u. Motoren-Fabrik Akt.-Ges. in Mannheim.

Verbrennungskraftmaschine mit Zündkammer.

Patentiert im Deutschen Reiche vom 18. März 1919 ab.

Gegenstand der Erfindung ist eine Verbrennungskraftmaschine mit hoher Verdichtung und Zündkammer, die mit dem Verdichtungsraum durch einen in den Zylinderkopf eingesetzten, als Verdampfer und Zünder dienenden Zündkörper verbunden ist. Bei allen bisher bekannt gewordenen Maschinen dieser Art ist der Zündkörper in den Zylinderkopf oder die Zündkammer so eingesetzt, daß er von allen Seiten von den Verbrennungsgasen umspült wird. Dies hat eine baldige Verbrennung, d. h. völlige Zerstörung des Einsatzkörpers zur Folge, wobei dessen häufig notwendig werdendes Auswechseln besondere Unkosten und Zeitverluste verursacht und es dennoch nicht verhütet werden kann, daß verbrannte Metallteilchen in den Zylinder gelangen und zerstörende Wirkungen auf die Kolbenlaufbahn ausüben. Diese Übelstände sollen bei der Erfindung dadurch behoben werden, daß der Zündkörper in den wassergekühlten Zylinderkopf so eingesetzt ist, daß nur seine Innenseite von den Verbrennungsgasen berührt wird. Zweckmäßig werden hierbei der Körper und die Bohrung, in die er als Futter eingesetzt ist, so ausgebildet, daß sich die Temperatur des Futters den jeweiligen Betriebsverhältnissen und dem jeweilig verwendeten Brennstoff durch Abändern der wärmeübertragenden Berührungsflächen leicht anpassen läßt. In der Praxis hat sich nämlich gezeigt, daß die Temperatur des Zündkörpers zur vollständigen Verdampfung bzw. Zerlegung und sicheren Zündung verschiedener Brennstoffe eine verschiedene sein muß, daß aber bei keinem der in

Betracht kommenden Brennstoffe eine so hohe Temperatur des Zündkörpers erforderlich ist, daß hierdurch dessen baldige Zerstörung bedingt wäre.

Aus dieser Erkenntnis ergab sich die den Gegenstand der Erfindung bildende Anordnung, bei der der Hohlkörper als eine Art Futter, zum Teil wärmeisoliert, in den wassergekühlten Verbindungskanal zwischen Zündkammer und Verdichtungsraum eingesetzt ist.

Man hat nun zwar schon bei Glühkopfmotoren den Glühkopf als Futter in den wassergekühlten Zylinderkopf eingesetzt, und zwar bei Motoren, bei welchen der Glühkopf mit seinem vollen Querschnitt — also ohne Hals — in den Verdichtungsraum einmündet. Bei Glühkopfmotoren bietet aber diese Anordnung nicht nur keine Vorteile, sondern sie ist durchaus unbrauchbar. Bekanntlich beträgt die Verdichtung bei dieser Motorenart höchstens 7 bis 8 Atmosphären, so daß die Zündung des Brennstoffs mehr durch die heißen Wandungen als durch die Verdichtungstemperatur erfolgt. Nun bereitet das Arbeiten bei schwacher Belastung schon bei normalen Glühkopfmotoren die größten Schwierigkeiten, weil der Glühkopf, der bei Vollast vielleicht kirschrot wird, sich bei schwacher Belastung so weit abkühlt, daß die Zündung der Ladung in Frage gestellt wird. Dieser Übelstand müßte bei Ausbildung des Glühkopfs als ein in den wassergekühlten Zylinderkopf eingesetztes Futter so stark auftreten, daß der Motor — falls man ihn überhaupt bei Vollast benutzen kann — bei schwächeren Belastungen ganz bestimmt versagen würde. Derartige Motoren haben sich deshalb in die Praxis nicht einführen können. Im Gegensatz hierzu beträgt die Verdichtung beim vorliegenden Hochdruckmotor zwischen 35 und 40 Atmosphären, so daß die Zündung des Brennstoffs mit Sicherheit durch die Verdichtungstemperatur bewirkt wird. Das in die Zündkammer eingesetzte Futter ist hier nur zur vollkommenen Verdampfung des durch die Düse aufgespritzten Brennstoffs erforderlich, die hier die sonst übliche Zerstäubung mittels Einblaseluft ersetzt. Da nun bei schwacher Belastung die auf den Einsatz gespritzte Brennstoffmenge geringer ist als bei Vollast, so ist im ersteren Falle auch die Wärmeentziehung beim Einsatz geringer als im zweiten Falle. Hierdurch wird die geringere Wärmezufuhr, die der Einsatz bei schwacher Belastung gegenüber Vollast erfährt, so weit ausgeglichen, daß der Motor — wie die Praxis gezeigt hat — bei allen Belastungen mit sicherer Zündung und guter Verbrennung arbeitet.

Auf der Zeichnung ist eine derartige An-

ordnung in einer beispielsweisen Ausführungsform dargestellt. Der Verdichtungsraum a des Zylinders steht mit der Zündkammer b durch den in den wassergekühlten Zylinderkopf eingesetzten Zündkörper c in Verbindung, welch letzterer zu diesem Zweck in seinem Boden mehrere Bohrungen d aufweist. Der Brennstoff wird durch die Düse e gegen Ende des Verdichtungshubes eingespritzt und trifft die Innenseite des Zündkörpers, wobei er an dessen heißen Wandungen verdampft und entzündet wird. Um mit Sicherheit zu erreichen, daß die gesamte eingespritzte Brennstoffmenge in den Zündkörper und nicht zum Teil gegen die Wandungen der Zündkammer gespritzt wird, ist der erstere an seinem der Zündkammer zugewendeten Ende trichterförmig erweitert. Am äußeren Umfang weist er an dieser Stelle einen zylindrischen Flansch f auf, der in der Bohrung g des Zylinderkopfes, in die der Zündkörper eingesetzt ist, genau paßt, so daß unterhalb des Flansches ein ringförmiger Raum h mit einer stillstehenden Luftschicht gebildet wird, die als Wärmeisolierung dient, wodurch der Zündkörper die erforderliche Temperatur annehmen kann. Der Ringraum kann jedoch auch mit Asbest, Kieselguhr oder einem anderen schlechten Wärmeleiter ausgefüllt sein. Die Temperatur, die der Zündkörper annimmt, hängt nun im wesentlichen von der wärmeübertragenden Berührungsfläche zwischen Flansch f und der Bohrung g ab. Man hat es also durch Wahl der Höhe des Flansches f in der Hand, die Temperatur des Zündkörpers zu verändern. Hält man mehrere derartige Hohlkörper mit verschiedener Flanschhöhe auf Lager, so können die günstigsten Bedingungen beim Übergang zu einem andern Brennstoff oder eine andere Drehzahl des Motors durch einfaches Auswechseln der Zündkörper in kürzester Zeit hergestellt werden.

PATENT-ANSPRUCH:

Verbrennungskraftmaschine mit hoher Verdichtung und Zündkammer, die mit dem Verdichtungsraum durch ein in den Zylinderkopf eingesetztes, als Verdampfer und Zünder dienendes Futter mittels eines oder mehrerer in diesem vorgesehenen engen Kanäle in Verbindung steht, dadurch gekennzeichnet, daß das Futter in den wassergekühlten Zylinderkopf derart eingesetzt ist, daß seine Außenseite mit Ausnahme des in bekannter Weise mit Zündkanälen versehenen Bodens gegen jeden Zutritt von Verbrennungsgasen dicht abgeschlossen und im oberen Teil von einem Isolierraum umgeben ist.

with Firing Chamber (Verbrennungs-kraftmaschine mit Zündkammer). The Reichspatentamt issued patent number 397,142, Klasse 46a, Gruppe 2, on March 18, 1919.

The basis for this invention was the transfer of fuel from the pre-combustion chamber to the main cylinder chamber by means of a funnel-shaped channel. The relatively high temperature of this insertion helped to vaporize the fuel without any carbon deposit. The construction of a marketable diesel engine with a pre-combustion chamber became now possible.

The possibility of constructing an engine suitable for vehicles was seriously considered and numerous studies were actually made on that subject. It was however decided to build a series of startionary units of 1, 2, 3, 4, and 6 cylinders. The first such small sized diesel engine of up to 15 horsepower per cylinder at 400 revolutions per minute was delivered to a customer on September 4, 1920. By the end of the year 1921, a total of over 200 such engines had been delivered and this type was then properly considered a successful addition to the engine manufacturing program of the company.

One of the results of the lost war was the rapidly deteriorating and even failing economic situation in the country despite all efforts of the government to stem the quick and totally ruinous inflation spiral.

The speedily rising prices had convinced the directors to concentrate on the manufacture of large, slow turning diesel engines suitable for marine purposes. L'Orange showed little or no inclination then to further advance the smaller vehicle engine development because he feared that if such an engine would become popular, the cost of fuel oil for all diesel engines would rise to such a point that it would have a retarding influence on all further diesel development. And there was just no capital available to finance costly testing without certain profitable returns.

In fact, the paramount concern of the Benz directors was their precarious financial situation. Many large and old-established companies were unable to continue operating and collapsed during this critical post-war period. Thus, when a newly formed consortium offered to buy the section dealing with the construction of the diesel engines, that is, The Division for Commercial and Stationary Engines, it was promptly sold to what was called the Motorenwerke Mannheim, usually known as MWM.

Report of engine test, May 14, 1921

Benz & Cie. Rheinische Automobil- u. Motoren-Fabrik Akt.-Ges. in Mannheim.

Einspritzdüse für Verbrennungskraftmaschinen.

Patentiert im Deutschen Reiche vom 10. Juli 1920 ab.

Gegenstand der Erfindung ist eine Düse von Verbrennungskraftmaschinen, bei denen der Brennstoff ohne Zuhilfenahme von Einblaseluft unmittelbar in den Zylinder eingestäubt wird.

Eine derartige Düse besteht im wesentlichen aus einem Nadelventil, das an dem der Nadel gegenüberliegenden Ende einen federbelasteten Kolben aufweist, der beim Druckhub der Brennstoffpumpe angehoben wird und das Nadelventil öffnet. Die Nadel hat bei kleineren Motoren nur einen Durchmesser von etwa 1 mm. Ihre genaue Zentrierung in dem zu ihrer Aufnahme an der Mündung der Düse gebohrten Loch gleichen Durchmessers bereitete bisher große Schwierigkeiten, weil das die erwähnte feine Bohrung aufweisende Stück in den Düsenkörper unmittelbar eingeschraubt wurde. Selbst auf der Drehbank geschnittene Verschraubungen ergeben aber nur zufällig eine genaue Zentrierung, die im vorliegenden Falle deshalb erforderlich ist, weil der erwähnte Steuerkolben der Nadel im Düsenkörper eingeschliffen ist und nicht im geringsten nachgeben kann. Die vorerwähnte Schwierigkeit wird durch den Erfindungsgegenstand dadurch behoben, daß das die erwähnte feine Bohrung aufweisende Stück ziemlich lose in den Düsenkörper eingesetzt ist und einen tellerventilartigen Sitz aufweist, der gegen einen entsprechenden Sitz des Düsenkörpers durch eine geeignete Verschraubung angepreßt wird. Hierdurch kann sich das Einsatzstück beim Anschrauben seitlich etwas verschieben und sich zur Nadel genau zentrisch einstellen.

Auf der beiliegenden Zeichnung ist eine solche Anordnung in einer beispielsweisen Ausführungsform schematisch dargestellt. Es bedeutet *a* den Düsenkörper, in den der Kolben *b* des Düsenventils dicht eingeschliffen und durch eine Feder *c* belastet ist. Das Düsenventil hat seinen Sitz in einem in den Düsenkörper eingesetzten Einsatzstück *d* (s. vergrößerte Zeichnung der Düsenmündung in Abb. 2), in dessen in den Zylinder führende Bohrung *e* eine feine Nadel *f* hineinragt. Um ein stets genau zentrisches Eindringen dieser Nadel in die Bohrung *e* zu erzielen, ist das Einsatzstück in den Düsenkörper ziemlich lose eingepaßt, so daß es sich seitlich nach allen Richtungen um ein weniges verschieben läßt. Es wird durch die in den Düsenkörper eindringende Verschraubung *g* vermittelst seines tellerartigen Sitzes *h* gegen eine entsprechende Sitzfläche des Düsenkörpers angepreßt und dadurch abgedichtet.

PATENT-ANSPRUCH:

Düse für Verbrennungskraftmaschinen, bei denen der Brennstoff ohne Zuhilfenahme von Einblaseluft unmittelbar in den Zylinder eingestäubt wird, wobei das mit einem in den Düsenkörper eingeschliffenen, federbelasteten Kolben versehene Düsenventil eine die Ausspritzöffnung teilweise verschließende Nadel aufweist, die beim Druckhub der Brennstoffpumpe angehoben wird, dadurch gekennzeichnet, daß das die Ausspritzöffnung aufweisende Einsatzstück nur lose in die Düse eingesetzt ist und einen tellerventilartigen Sitz aufweist, vermittels dessen es durch eine Verschraubung gegen eine entsprechende Sitzfläche des Düsenkörpers angepreßt wird und sich hierbei genau zentrisch zur Nadel einstellen kann.

Hierzu 1 Blatt Zeichnungen.

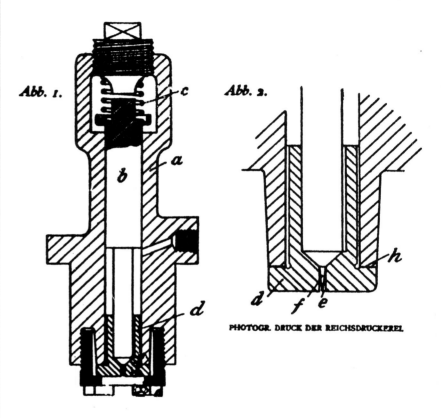

Abb. 1. Abb. 2.

PHOTOGR. DRUCK DER REICHSDRUCKEREI

Other patent documents pertaining to injection nozzles, to regulation of fuel pumps, and to connection lines between combustion chamber and cylinder chambers

Man unterscheidet zwei Arten von Regulierungen für die Brennstoffpumpen von Verbrennungskraftmaschinen: Die Präzisionsregulierungen und die ungesteuerte Rücklaufregulierung. Zu der ersteren Gattung gehören diejenigen Regulierungen, durch die dem Zylinder für den Verbrennungsvorgang eine ganz bestimmte, der jeweiligen Einstellung des Regulierorgans entsprechende Menge Brennstoff zugeführt wird, unabhängig davon, ob der Motor mit einer hohen oder einer niedrigen Drehzahl läuft. Diese Regulierung kann z. B. durch Veränderung des Hubes des Pumpenkolbens erzielt werden oder durch veränderliche, zwangläufi...

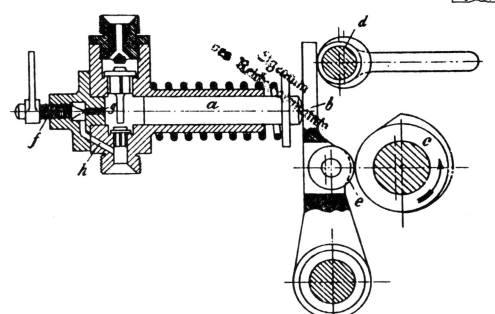

Gegenstand der vorliegenden Erfindung ist eine Brennstoffpumpe für Verbrennungskraftmaschinen, bei denen der Brennstoff ohne Zuhilfenahme von Einblaseluft unmittelbar in den Verdichtungsraum bzw. in eine Zündkammer eingespritzt wird. Die Pumpe arbeitet in der Weise, daß der Pumpenkolben mittels eines Nockens angehoben wird, auf den ihn eine starke Feder scharf anpreßt. Zwischen Pumpenkolben und Nocken ist ein Hebel zwischengeschaltet, der in bekannter Weise mittels eines Exzenters verstellt werden kann.

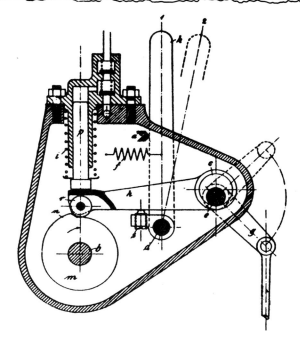

27

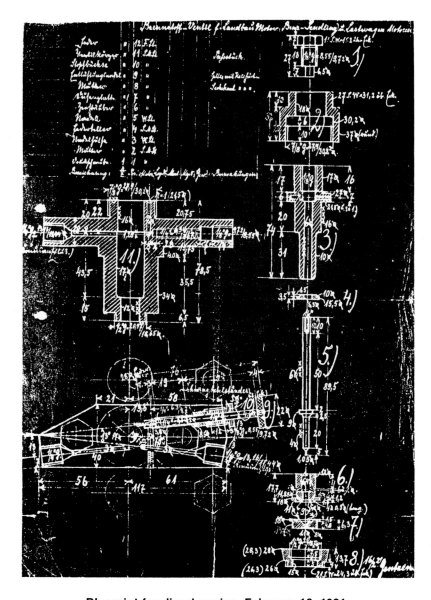

Blueprint for diesel engine, February 16, 1921

One of the conditions of the sale stipulated that the purchasers were allowed to build diesel engines incorporating the pre-chamber principles covered by the Benz patents, but the manufacture of all diesel engines weighing under 25 kilograms per horsepower remained with the Benz & Cie. The construction of these smaller and lighter diesel engines was planned for their factory at Waldhof.

Years before the Benz company had signed a contract with the Motorenfabrik München-Sendling, manufacturers of three-wheeled farm tractors and motor-plows agreeing to supply engines. They planned to replace the current 25-horsepower gasoline engine with a diesel engine, and the rather substantial fuel cost saving was expected to be an added incentive to sales of this farm implement. In January 1922 the first two-cylinder 30-horsepower (at 800 revolutions per minute) diesel engines were completed and installed into the motor plow to be delivered to customers. A separate sales organization, the Benz-Sendling Motorplow Sales Company, was founded. Two motor-plows were exhibited at the *Landwirtschaftlichen Ausstellung der Deutschen Ostmesse* (Agricultural Exposition of the German East Fair) at Königsberg in June 1922. The first machine was sold to a *Rittergut* (estate farms) in Trömpau at 165 million marks during this time when inflation ran wild in Germany. The sales were so encouraging that on March 6, 1923 it was decided to manufacture a series of one hundred units. A concentrated sales effort was organized in August of that year.

The diesel unit was similar to the Leissner type engine (with the ignition paper) although the engine had a lower compression ratio and other minor alterations. This tractor engine was duly noted and carefully examined by the British firm of McLaren of Leeds, builders of two-engined gang plows. Their need was for two engines of at least 60 horsepower output. To supply them, Benz decided to build a four-cylinder engine, similar to that of the two-cylinder type, as a regular production model. This engine quickly found, in addition to the use in the tractor, other uses, such as for mining cars, movable compressor units, electric auxiliary units, marine engines, as well as the former uses of the two-cylinder powerplants. The production series was then extended to include a three- and six-cylinder engine as well. Higher power output was achieved by increasing the engine revolutions and making other improvements. (All manufacture of these engines was eventually transferred in 1950 to the Marienfelder factory of the Daimler-Benz company.)

378174

Benz & Cie. Rheinische Automobil- und Motoren-Fabrik A. G. in Mannheim.

Rückdruckfrei regelbare Brennstoffpumpe für Verbrennungskraftmaschinen.

Patentiert im Deutschen Reiche vom 26. Juli 1921 ab.

Gegenstand der Erfindung ist eine Regelung von Brennstoffpumpen für Einspritzverbrennungskraftmaschinen, bei denen der Brennstoff ohne Zuhilfenahme von Einblaseluft unmittelbar in den Zylinder bzw. in eine Zündkapsel eingespritzt wird. Der Pumpenkolben wird mittelbar durch einen Nocken betätigt, gegen den er durch eine Feder angedrückt wird. Die Förderleistung der Pumpe wird durch einen Regler beeinflußt, der die Steuerung der Pumpe entsprechend verstellt. Bei dem im Motor verwirklichten Verfahren und der dadurch bedingten Arbeitsweise der Pumpe muß nun ganz besonders vermieden werden, daß ein Rückdruck auf das Reglergestänge ausgeübt wird. Die Pumpe arbeitet mit sehr hohen Drücken und dabei entstehen bei der kurzen Einspritzdauer sehr starke Stöße, die naturgemäß nicht zum Regler weitergeleitet werden dürfen; auch wird durch einen starken Rückdruck auf das Reglergestänge das Verstellen der Pumpe sehr erschwert.

Man hat nun schon versucht, den Rückdruck dadurch auszuschalten, daß man einen Kolbenschieber durch den Regler verstellen läßt. Eine derartige Schlitzsteuerung läßt sich aber mit der Änderung der Förderleistung durch wechselnden Pumpenhub kaum vereinigen. Ein zweiter Weg ist der, daß man selbstsperrende Elemente, wie Keil oder Schraube, in den Mechanismus zur Übertragung der Verstellbewegung des Reglers einschaltet. Derartige Vorrichtungen sind naturgemäß immer ziemlich kompliziert und lassen sich praktisch kaum ohne etwas toten Gang ausführen. Sie weisen zahlreiche Gelenkstellen auf, haben große Reibungsverluste und bedingen demzufolge einen stärkeren Regler.

Nach der Erfindung ist nun die Aufgabe mit einfachsten Mitteln dadurch gelöst, daß

durch die Formgebung des Pumpennockens und die Ausbildung der Pumpensteuerung ein Gegendruck überhaupt nicht entstehen kann. Die Pumpe arbeitet in der Weise, daß der Pumpenkolben mittels einer kräftigen Feder stark gegen das eine Ende eines Winkelhebels angepreßt wird, dessen anderes Ende mittels einer Rolle auf einer Scheibe ruht. Letztere trägt einen Nocken, der bei seinem Auftreffen auf die Rolle des Winkelhebels den Pumpenkolben schlagartig betätigt. Der Hub und damit die Leistung der Pumpe kann nun in der Weise verändert werden, daß der Drehpunkt des Winkelhebels verlegt und damit die Rolle von der Nockenscheibe entfernt oder ihr genähert wird. Der Antrieb des Pumpenkolbens mittels eines Winkelhebels und die Verschiebung des Drehpunktes des Winkelhebels sind schon früher ausgeführt oder vorgeschlagen worden. Nach der Erfindung werden nun die ansteigende Bahn des Nockens und die beiden Schenkel des Winkelhebels so gestaltet und bemessen, daß die Bahnnormale des Nockens durch den Angriffspunkt des Winkelhebels am Brennstoffpumpenkolben geht.

Der der Erfindung zugrunde liegende Gedanke soll an zwei Ausführungsbeispielen erläutert werden. Bei der in Abb. 1 dargestellten Konstruktion bezeichnet a den Abstand des Drehpunktes des Winkelhebels von der Rolle, h die Länge des zweiten Winkelhebelarmes, V, die Vertikalkomponente und H, die Horizontalkomponente der vom Nocken erzeugten Kraft P. Der Winkel α der ansteigenden Nockenbahn gegen die Horizontale ist so gewählt, daß die Vertikalkomponente V, größer ist als Horizontalkomponente H, α ist der Winkel der ansteigenden Nockenbahn und zugleich der Winkel, den der auf den Pumpenkolben wirkende Hebelarm als Kathete des

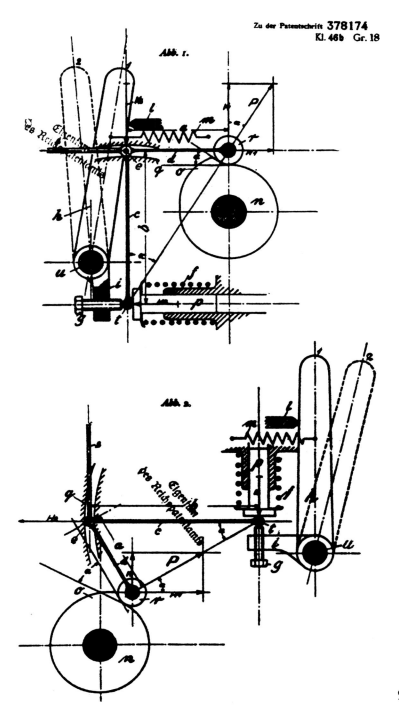

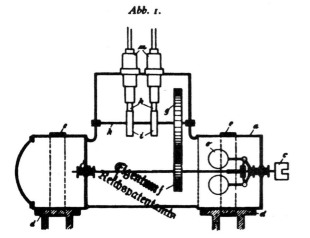

Abb. 1.

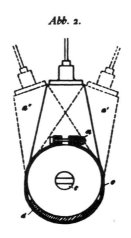

Abb. 2.

Bei Verbrennungsmotoren mit Zündkammer steht diese durch enge Verbindungskanäle mit dem Zylinderraum in Verbindung. Diese Kanäle haben den Zweck, die Kammer in bestimmtem Grade vom Zylinderinnern abzuschnüren, so daß beim Verdichtungshub der Druck in der Kammer hinter dem im Zylinderraum zurückbleibt. Die Einspritzung erfolgt kurz vor Totpunkt, und nun entsteht am Anfang des folgenden Arbeitshubes infolge der einsetzenden Verbrennung ein Überdruck in der Kammer gegenüber dem Zylinderinnern. Der Druckunterschied in der Kammer bewirkt bei der Verdichtung das Durchwirbeln des Zündkammerinhaltes und die Verteilung des eingespritzten Brennstoffes durch den Luftstrom aus dem Zylinder und damit eine solche Gemischbildung in der Kammer, daß in dieser eine möglichst vollkommene Verbrennung stattfindet. Durch die Verbrennung entsteht ein Überdruck in

dünn werden, so daß die Gefahr schlechter Wärmeableitung und dadurch des Verzunderns vorliegt.

Nach der Erfindung werden die Verbindungskanäle in zwei oder mehr Reihen angeordnet, um die Zahl der Öffnungen in jeder Reihe möglichst klein zu halten und damit die Stegdicke zwischen den Bohrungen in jeder Reihe möglichst groß zu machen. Andererseits werden die Kegel, auf welchen die Bohrungen jeder Reihe liegen, so gewählt, daß die Kegelwinkel von der untersten Reihe nach den oberen fortschreitend immer spitzer werden, so daß die Stegstärken zwischen benachbarten Verbindungskanälen in verschiedenen Reihen von außen nach innen nicht so schnell wie bei den älteren Ausführungen abnehmen. Es wird auf diese Weise zunächst erreicht, daß für die Wärmeabführung zwischen den Bohrungen größere Wandstärken zur Verfügung stehen, was die Wärmeabfüh-

Abb. 1.

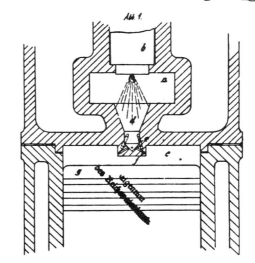

Abb. 2.

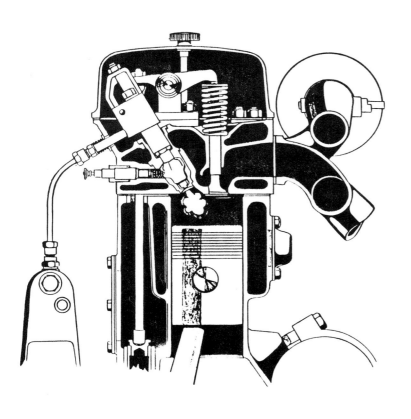

Other patent documents pertaining to injection nozzles,
to regulation of fuel pumps, and to connection lines between
combustion chamber and cylinder chambers

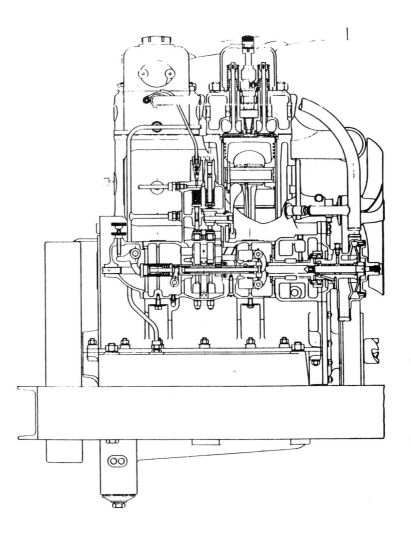

With their tractor engine well accepted and production under way, it was decided to construct one for commercial vehicles. This lighter-weight four-cylinder diesel engine was to be exchangeable with the gasoline engine powering the five-ton truck and should produce about 50 horsepower at a higher rate of engine revolutions.

After Prosper L'Orange had left the company in 1921, Kurt Eltze took over the further development work on the diesel engine, specifically to create a suitable engine for smaller vehicles. The basic measurements of the gasoline engines were to be maintained. The running gear and the arrangement of the four individual upright cylinders was taken over in its entirety. But the valve activation mechanism was enclosed to protect it against dust. The regulation of the injection pump was redesigned by the constructor Polatscheck in cooperation with Gentzen and Eltze, so that the camshaft now regulated the fuel supply cams, making higher revolutions for the vehicle engine possible.

Although at the earliest times of the internal combustion engine period, the pioneers Karl Benz and Gottlieb Daimler had developed their own ignition systems, when Robert Bosch created an especially constructed system which proved superior to all others then existing, these two automobile manufacturers ceased building their own units. The Bosch company consistently provided a superior product and it was but natural for these specialists to develop also a better ignition system for the pre-combustion chamber diesel engine. Thus, when in 1922 Benz, Henschel and MAN showed considerable success with their respective diesel engines for vehicles, Bosch devised a glow plug to provide the initial spark. This device was appreciably preferrable to the cumbersome paper method to start a cold engine, so that it was quickly adopted instead.

Engine tests were made on January 25, 1923, and proved satisfactory. Fuel consumption was 240 grams per horsepower, about 25 percent less than a similar gasoline engine. In February an OB type engine was installed into the truck and tests began in September. On a 103-kilometer test drive the truck used 32 percent less fuel and saved 86 percent in costs, Eltze reported to an assembly on December 20, 1923.

The first Benz-built diesel-engined truck was shown at the Automobile Show at Amsterdam on February 4, 1924, where it created tremendous interest. It was a five-ton truck with propeller shaft drive,

Benz-Sendling-Motorpflüge G. m. b. H., Berlin NW 7, Unter den Linden 57/58. [*34a/271*].

45. **Motorpflug Type S 7** (Abb. 20) (8 D. R. P. und 17 D. R. G. M.). Brennstoff: Lampenpetroleum. — Einradantrieb in der Mitte des Fahrzeuges. — Die Kippgefahr beim Arbeiten am Hang wird vermieden durch seitlich ausschwenkbare Stützräder. — Vereinfachter Zweizylinder-Dieselmotor. Bohrung: 135, Hub: 200 mm. — Drehzahl: 800. — Bremsleistung: 30 PS. — Brennstoffverbrauch je PS/Std.: 220 g. — Brennstoff- und Luftfilter vorhanden. Kupplung: Gußeiserne Reibscheibe, Patent Benn. — Ein Vorwärts-, ein Rückwärtsgang. — Vorwärtsgeschwindigkeiten durch Auswechseln der Kettenräder zwischen 3 und 4 km abstufbar. — Riemenscheibe

Above and left: Detailed description of S7 plow and two other types. *Below:* During inflation, the price was 177 million marks, with attachments.

vorhanden.
Breite 170
hinten 140
Gewicht

c 4710,
m 850,
00 mm.

Motor plow prospectus of Agricultural Fair, Hamburg, 1924

Wir/Ich gebe—Ihnen auf Grund der beiliegenden Lieferungsbedingungen hiermit in Auftrag

Benz-Sendling-Motorpflug

Ihrem Katalog entsprechend.

Derselbe besteht aus: einem Benz-Sendling-Motorschlepper und einem 3scharigen Kultur-Anhängepflug. beides mit den normalen Zubehör und Reserveteilen ausgerüstet, sowie einem Satz Pflugscharen, einem Rundsech und einem Stoßfänger.

Der Preis des Schleppers beträgt heute . . . . ℳ

Der Preis des 3scharigen Kulturpfluges . . . . ℳ

zusammen ℳ

Ferner bestelle ich noch hinzu:

ℳ

ℳ

ℳ

ℳ

Benz 30-horsepower two-cylinder diesel engine, 1922

powered by the pre-combustion chamber diesel engine of 50 horsepower at 1,000 revolutions per minute.

The value and importance of this diesel truck was recognized by the domestic and foreign automotive writers. Even in the press of the United States, where diesel-powered vehicles appeared years later than in Germany, this new construction received considerable comment. The success of the pre-combustion chamber system made several domestic and foreign companies acquire licenses to manufacture engines based on that principle. Later on, several law suits resulted over these patents but the priority of the Benz patent was sustained by the courts.

The OB2 engine had a bore of 125 millimeters and a stroke of 180 millimeters, separate vertical cylinders and overhead inlet and exhaust valves actuated by a camshaft housed on the left side of the engine and the usual pushrods and rocker arms. Arranged on the same side was the Benz injection pump in combination with a centrifugal governor which the driver could regulate for any engine speed required.

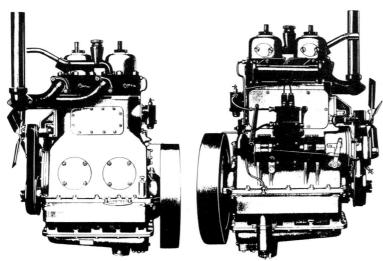

First diesel engine, 30-32 hp, built for vehicle, 1922

Benz OB four-cylinder diesel engine of 45 horsepower for 5-ton truck, 1923

At the Daimler Works in Marienfelde, after years of extensive testing, a truck engine using the fuel-blowing system, had also been developed under the guidance of Friedrich Schwarz. Tests with a 3.5-ton truck and total weight of 7.680 kilograms on the road from Berlin to Stuttgart and back showed fuel consumption of 200 to 250 grams per horsepower for the 40-horsepower (at 1,000 revolutions per minute) diesel engine. And at the Automobile Show at Berlin in October 1923 three such diesel-powered vehicles had been exhibited. But when in 1924 the first merger talks between Benz and Daimler took place, eventually terminating in a complete merger of all facilities in 1926, this system was discontinued. All production of diesel engines used the superior pre-combustion chamber Benz system.

In 1924 the Bosch company acquired a Benz truck, powered by the 50-horsepower diesel engine, for experimental purposes. The research activities at their laboratories were accelerated, and the following year the rights to the Acro-aircompression engine including the injection pump and pin nozzle, invented by Franz Lang, were also obtained. (Acro stood for American Crude Oil Corporation, at Küssnacht.) This Lang injection pump which contained, besides the pump piston, a steering piston with slanting edges as pusher, was so simplified by Bosch that both pistons could be combined. This extraordinary simplification made the Bosch injection pump the standard construction system. The fuel could be injected at higher revolutions and better controlled than in the Benz construction. When this new Bosch system was available in 1927, Benz ceased all further development and constuction work on their pumps and atomizers.

In 1927 Benz, but actually the merged Daimler-Benz company, in their Mannheim truck plant, built a six-cylinder diesel engine of 75-horsepower (at 1,300 revolutions per minute) for the OM 5 truck of five-ton load capacity. The first of these models was delivered on January 19, 1928, to a Melbourne customer, the second one in July to a London client. The *Glasgow Herald* reported in November of that year that the Dewar Trophy was awarded to that truck engine for the Best Achivement of the Year. In Germany several fine test results created a demand for this type vehicle and it was put into large series production.

The post-war period of economic disaster was also a most burdensome and insecure time for all of the eighty-six automobile manufacturers in Germany who built a total of 144 models of passenger cars. Not only the raging inflation but also the punitive luxury tax of 15 percent of the purchase price of an automobile contributed to the serious survival problem of the manufacturers.

The Daimler and Benz merger resulted in a curtailment of their own passenger car model production and commercial vehicles and duplication of model types underwent sharp reduction at the former Daimler Marienfelde and Benz Mannheim plants where the diesel engines were built.

However, the production of diesel engines by the Daimler com-

Diesel Engine Used in New Benz Truck

BENZ & CO. of Mannheim has announced details concerning its new 5-ton truck fitted with a Diesel engine. Two views of the powerplant of this truck are shown herewith. The engine works on the true Diesel cycle, using a compression pressure of slightly over 500 lb. p. sq. in., the fuel charge being ignited by heat generated by the compression of the air.

No air compressor plant for injection purposes is used. The system of fuel injection seems to be similar to that employed in the Hvid engine. There is an ignition chamber on top of the cylinder, in which a small quantity of the fuel ignites spontaneously and forces the rest of the fuel into the combustion chamber in the form of a very fine spray.

It is claimed that the Benz-Diesel engine can be operated on any heavy fuel such as crude oil; that the engine can be idled for any length of time and that it will carry a full load immediately after an extended period of idling.

In external appearance this powerplant does not differ materially from the conventional truck engine. The individual cylinders have both the inlet and the exhaust valves in the head, which are inclosed under an aluminum cover and operated by outside pushrods. The ignition chamber is arranged between the two valves. As is customary in engines of this type, the cylinder heads are cast separately. The engine is fitted with a centrifugal governor, a Bosch electric starting motor driving the flywheel and a preheating tank for the fuel in the upper tank of the radiator. Lubrication is by pressure.

Starting of the engine is effected in two stages and usually by means of the electric starter. During the first stage the exhaust valves are lifted and their seats by means of a hand lever. The starting motor then cranks the engine over rapidly and the flywheel accumulates momentum. After a sufficient speed has been attained the exhaust valves are released by the hand lever, but they are prevented from closing entirely by small auxiliary cams.

The result is that during the early part of the compression stroke a certain amount of the air which has been drawn in escapes again and the compression therefore is kept below its value in normal operation. Consequently, not sufficient heat is developed by the compression during this stage of the starting operation to ignite the charge spontaneously, and ignition is effected by means of an ignition plug which carries a filament which is maintained in an incandescent state by means of current from a storage battery.

After the first ignition the camshaft is shifted axially into its normal working position, whereby the auxiliary cams are put out of action and the current is cut off from the ignition plug. Thereafter ignition takes place entirely automatically.

The engine has four cylinders of substantially 5 in. bore and 7⅛ in. stroke, and is claimed to develop 50 hp. at 1000 r.p.m. The fuel consumption is given as 0.53 lb. p. hp.-h.

TWO new alloys have been introduced in aircraft engine construction by the Engineering Division of the Air Service, McCook Field. One is a light structural alloy containing 93 per cent magnesium, 5 per cent aluminum and 2 per cent zinc, and is used for the crankcase of a W-type aircraft engine, resulting in a saving in weight of something like 200 lb. as compared with the aluminum alloy containing 8 per cent of copper, which was previously used.

The other alloy consists of aluminum, copper, nickel and magnesium, and while the formula is not new, being of the duralumin class, the heat treatment has been improved and increased mechanical qualities secured as a result. One of the valuable properties of this alloy is said to be that it retains its strength at high temperatures, which is of value because it is used principally for such parts as engine cylinders, pistons, cylinder heads and manifolds.

First report on Benz diesel truck in the American periodical *Automotive Industries* of March 16, 1924

pany was an important and substantial part of the history of that company, despite the fact that the Benz pre-combustion chamber design was selected as the superior system for all diesel engines to be produced after the merger.

Soon after the first relatively heavy and slow-turning large stationary diesel engines became generally accepted, the Daimler Motoren Gesellschaft had decided to construct diesel engines, but as small as those using gasoline as fuel. The *Einblaseverfahren* (blowing-in system) of fuel by compressed air into the cylinder had been chosen by that company. The development work was directed by Kurt Eltze, who had come to work at the Marienfelde Works. This engine building company was taken over by the Daimler company in 1902, and the factory was used solely for the manufacture of stationary engines from then on, even after the merger with Benz.

The first diesel marine engines, developing 60 and 100 horsepower, were built in 1912. Larger and heavier stationary engines, suitable for dynamo work, soon followed and by 1914 engines developing 175 and 260 horsepower were produced. A year later, a

Benz OM5 six-cylinder truck diesel engine of 1927

series of smaller six-cylinder diesel engines followed, but developing 300 horsepower at 500 revolutions per minute, then considered a rather high rate of engine speed. Another series of still greater power output engines of 550 horsepower at 450 revolutions per minute were followed by diesel engines suitable for installations in submarines. Those were six-cylinder units which developed as much as 1,700 horsepower at 380 revolutions per minute.

Experimental work was conducted during 1913 on smaller diesel engines, using the system where the fuel was forced by air pressure directly into the combustion chamber. The experience with some thirty engines of 5, 8, 10, and 14 horsepower output led to the adaption of fuel injection by an injection pump. An engine of this type was actually exhibited at the Agricultural Show at Hannover in 1914, and another was built and installed in a tractor.

After the disruption caused by the war, the diesel development work was again resumed by the engineers under Kurt Eltze at the Marienfelde works, but now based on their air injection system. In 1921, three four-cylinder engines with a bore of 110 millimeters and stroke of

Benz 5-ton truck with OB diesel, 1923

150 millimeters and developing 40 horsepower at 1,000 revolutions per minute were built for testing purposes.

An engine of this type was installed into a four-ton bus equipped with propeller shaft drive. Towards the end of 1922 and early the next year, various extensive tests were carried out on the road. The results were promising and consequently the trials were extended and intensified. During August of 1923 a truck with a 3-ton payload was test driven from Berlin to Frankfurt-on-the-Oder, a distance of some 90 kilometers (about 55 miles). During the trip the engine ran smoothly and adapted itself well to the changing road conditions and gradients as well as to load variations, although the driving speed did not exceed 25 miles per hour. After these tests were satisfactorily completed, a truck, a three-way tipper, and a bus were exhibited at the Berlin Automobile Show in October 1923. These were the first diesel-engined utility vehicles shown publicly anywhere.

Thus, the pioneering ground work had been laid for a diesel engine suitable for a passenger car by the two companies, working independently and each developing a successful, light-weight, fast-turning vehicle engine. Now, with the separate experiences of the two able engineering staffs combined into one operating unit, it was a foregone conclusion that the ultimate goal, to create such a smaller diesel engine, would be achieved soon.

Daimler 40-horsepower diesel engine in truck, 1923

*   *   *   *   *

When the *Automobil Ausstellung* in the huge Berlin Charlottenburg exposition halls opened its doors to the public in October, 1923, thousands of automobile enthusiasts—among them this fourteen-year old boy—crowded the aisles to feast on the excitingly magnificent cars exhibited. Surely not many of the spectators ever hoped to own even one of the smallest automobiles shown; just to imagine sitting behind the wheel of one was enough rapture to contemplate. But aside from the beautiful passenger cars, the more significant exhibit was found in the commercial vehicle section of the show. Mercedes exhibited three vehicles—two trucks and a bus—powered by the newly developed diesel engine.

This noteworthy event heralded the beginning of a new era for commercial vehicles and suggested the new method for equipping passenger cars with these more economical engines.

Dewar Trophy for "Best Achievement of the Year," 1928

Mercedes-Benz Diesel Automobiles

380 tests

In March 1933 General Director Wilhelm Kissel of Daimler-Benz expressed publicly the hope that a reasonably priced six-passenger car, powered by a diesel engine, could be developed in time for the prestigious Berlin Automobile Show the following year, "to instill new life into the precarious passenger car situation."

He also urged strongly that all further passenger automobiles should be so constructed that they could easily be fitted with either a gasoline or a diesel engine. This would mean greater tensile strength with consequently an increase in total weight of the heavier construction cars (with greater engine weight and stronger components, such as clutch, drive units, transmission and rear axle), as the chief engineer pointed out.

Work began under the guidance of Hans Nibel, who had been active at Benz since 1904 and had led the development work of diesel truck engines since 1922, and was then chief engineer at the Untertürkheim works since January 1929. The actual construction work and testing was done by Hermann Apel—later engineer Scharf assisted in that work—all under the close supervision of Eckhart Schmidt.

The six-cylinder engine displaced 3.8 liters, had a bore of 92 millimeters and stroke of 100 millimeters and developed between 80 and 82 horsepower at a maximum revolution of 2,800 per minute. This signified a definite improvement over earlier diesel engines. The Dechamps unit of 1910 ran at 800, and the Cummins unit of 1930 reached 1,000 to 1,200 revolutions per minute. The Mercedes-Benz diesel engine of 1934 reached those of a gasoline engine and developed about 21.5 horsepower per liter displacement, actually a quite remarkable achievement. (The 170D engine reached 23.5 and the 180D had 22.6 horsepower, many years later.)

After considerable bench-testing which had begun in September 1933, the 3.8-liter diesel engine was mounted in a chassis of the Mercedes-Benz Mannheim 370 model, a regular production car with the 3.7-liter gasoline engine of 75 horsepower. Driven on the spacious factory grounds and the surrounding country area, it was found that this diesel unit caused far too much vibration. Despite all efforts by the engineers to eliminate this damaging effect on the chassis, the problem could not be satisfactorily solved.

Therefore, the anticipated regular series production of the projected diesel model was abandoned and the original intention of exhibiting this very first Mercedes-Benz diesel-engined passenger car at the Berlin Automobile Show of March 1934 was cancelled. However, further development work was continued, particularly when various successful tests at the Gaggenau factory strengthened the belief of the chief designers that their work would eventually meet with success.

Instead of trying to develop a fast turning diesel engine for passenger cars, as the Untertürkheim engineers did, the men at the Gaggenau plant worked on a lighter slow-turning diesel engine suitable for such automobiles. Their purpose was not to develop the truck engine for the passenger cars, but to demonstrate that such an engine was indeed suitable for installation in a regular sedan. In this "friendly

**Hans Nibel,
Chief Engineer,
1929-1934**

Left: the 1929 Mannheim 370 model, 15/75 horsepower gasoline-engined. **Above:** the 1931 Nürburg 500 model, 19/100 horsepower gasoline-engined.

competition" between the two factories, an OM 67 six-cylinder diesel engine with a bore of 110 millimeters and stroke of 130 millimeters, and developing 95 horsepower at 2,000 revolutions per minute, was installed in a Mercedes-Benz Nürburg 500 model. This regular production model was built for the 4.9-liter gasoline engine of 110 horsepower. The diesel version was driven by the project engineer Bockemüller in a 100-mile distance test drive from Gaggenau to Untertürkheim.

The hoped-for introduction of the diesel engine into passenger cars was, of course, not without considerable risk and generated some adverse criticism. And now the strenuous efforts made to accomplish such an unorthodox initial adaptation had come to nothing. The vast experience in diesel engine manufacture at Daimler-Benz had created the strong belief that the economic and technical difficulties which existed could easily be overcome, although a practical and suitable

design for mass production had so far not appeared anywhere at competing car manufactures either.

The brief statement made by the Daimler-Benz directors at the time indicated that the company was fairly optimistic regarding the future of diesel-engined automobiles: "The diesel engine program, which our company in particular has dealt with so successfully up until now in its pioneering work with heavy and light commercial vehicles, is one which is uppermost in our minds and has priority in our development work. The ways in which the diesel engine could be employed are by no means exhausted. Strenuous efforts will, however, be necessary in order to develop the diesel passenger car into a vehicle of the highest quality."

The failure of this initial effort to bring that about was diplomatically not mentioned in this official statement, although the facts were public knowledge among automotive journalists and automobile manufacturing companies.

Model 260D

Hans Nibel, who had been chief at the Berlin Marienfelde plant since 1926 became chief engineer of the company upon the death of Max Sailer in November 1934. With the co-operation of the able engineers, Fritz Nallinger and Albert Hess, the problems of the diesel-engined passenger car were then successfully solved and the project was carried through to a satisfactory conclusion.

After the original project with the 3.8-liter six-cylinder diesel engine had been definitely abandoned, the engineers at the Untertürkheim plant concentrated on the construction of a new 2.6-liter four-cylinder unit. It was believed that the available horsepower of such a smaller power plant would prove adequate for a passenger car. And the individual cylinders were of the identical size—thought then the ideal displacement—as those of the former six-cylinder 3.8-liter engine, having a bore of 90 millimeters and stroke of 100 millimeters. (The original displacement of 2.53 liters was increased to 2.6 liters before serious testing began.)

At the same time a three-cylinder unit was also constructed, but that engine was not even tested when initial trial results with the other proved most promising.

The problem of achieving a decided reduction in the weight of an engine of this kind, mainly because of the high compression ratio which necessitated heavier construction of many parts, was still quite puzzling. Reliability was one of the major concerns and yet excessive weight would be a great handicap in achieving the desired economy of operation. There were also no easy solutions to the vexing problems of how to make the unit more flexible and to achieve smoother running of it. This was essential to fulfill the demands of all driving conditions.

The advantages of the pre-combustion chamber system were most strongly desired with diesel engines for passenger cars because the injection pressure, compared with the other systems, could be lowered, thus sparing the engine as well as the injection equipment. The resulting final smooth combustion process eliminated jerky stresses on the bearings and moving parts. Consequently the engine ran more quietly, practically without smoke, and also more economically, even when partly loaded. The engineers hoped that the quiet running of the diesel engine could still be further improved.

Eventually the combustion chamber configuration was somewhat altered and the problems of fuel injection, that is, pumps, nozzles, and power control, were all successfully solved in cooperation with Robert Bosch engineers. In fact, the injection unit was of Bosch manufacture.

After all of the preliminary experimental testing work was satisfactorily completed, the OM 138 four-cylinder diesel engine, producing 45 horsepower at 3,000 revolutions per minute with a compression ratio of 20.5 to 1, was installed in a slightly reinforced W138 production sedan chassis which normally was fitted with the 2.3-liter gasoline engine.

The vehicle reached a maximum speed of 97 kilometers (60.3 miles) per hour. The average fuel consumption was merely 9.5 liters per 100 kilometers of driving (24.7 miles per gallon). To facilitate starting, a 12 volt battery was fitted and a glow plug provided good response.

After long and exhaustive testing on the road, the car was adjudged ready for the regular production line and official public introduction. This relatively heavy automobile was intended to be used primarily as a taxicab, or even light delivery van, but the good qualities of the 260D model contributed immensely to the rapid use as a private passenger automobile.

At the Berlin Automobile Show (actually the *"Internationale Kraftfahrzeug-Ausstellung"*) in February 1936, the 260D created a sensa-

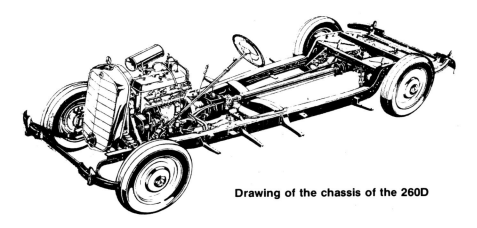

Drawing of the chassis of the 260D

Upper right: the four-cylinder 45-horsepower diesel engine. *Above:* the OM138 diesel engine in the chassis of the 260D, injection side. *Right:* the OM138 diesel engine in the chassis with the transmission.

tion. It was the first regular production diesel-engined automobile. Fitted with a landaulet style body, commonly used on taxis at that time, this car actually represented a further step in the development that began with the Benz pre-combustion chamber design and its most successful employment in Daimler-Benz engines for heavier commercial vehicles. (On April 6, 1935, the 10,000th diesel-engined commercial vehicle had been built by the company.)

An American observer reported that "the automobile was rougher than a gasoline-powered car at lower speeds, but at a speed of between 50 and 60 kilometers (31 to 38 miles) per hour it ran smoothly and one could not differentiate if one sat behind a diesel or gasoline-engined vehicle."

The 260D four-door sedan had a wheelbase of 3,050 millimeters (120 inches) and an overall length of 4,800 millimeters (189 inches). The height was 1,600 millimeters (63 inches) and width was 1,710 millimeters (67.3 inches) with a ground clearance of 200 millimeters (8.7 inches). The total weight was about 1,600 kilograms (3,520 pounds), with the chassis weighing about 1,100 kilograms (2,420 pounds).

The diesel models were identical to the gasoline-powered ones and had the swing axle, oil pressure four-wheel brakes, fully synchronized gears, one-pressure lubricating system, and such refinements which the discriminating buyer of a Mercedes-Benz automobile expected.

The OM 138 four-cylinder diesel engine had a bore of 90 millimeters (3.54 inches) and stroke of 100 millimeters (3.94 inches), actually displacing 2,545 cubic centimeters (but for tax rating purposes it was considered 2,527 cubic centimeters). The overhead camshaft engine had a five-bearing crankshaft, and light metal pistons. Maximum speed was about 95 kilometers (59.3 miles) per hour, according to the stop watch, but 100 kilometers (62.4 miles) per hour was generally quoted. Constant cruising speed was 90 kilometers (56 miles) per hour for autobahn travel. The rear axle ratio was 4.03 to 1. Fuel consumption was rated at 9 to 11 liters per 100 kilometers (about 24 miles per gallon), and oil consumption was given as 0.25 liters for 100 kilometers of driving.

The fuel tank held 50 liters (13.2 gallons) with a reserve of 4 liters, which could be activated by a switch on the dashboard. The batteries furnished were two of 62.5 ampere/hours each, but generally stated as 12 volt capacity of 105 ampere/hours. The cooling system held about 11 liters. Tires were 6.50×15.

Above: **the 260D landaulet of 1935.** *Below:* **the 260D sedan of 1935.**

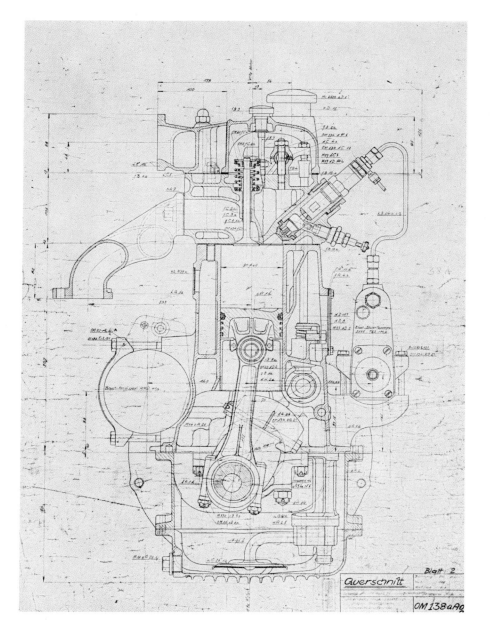

Querschnitt

Blatt 2

OM 138 aAg

The 260D sedan of 1937

The 260D was available in sedan style for five passengers, with or without sunroof, at DM 6,800 (sunroof: DM 235. extra), as six-passenger pullman limousine, with or without sunroof (cost: DM 280.) for DM 7,600., as six-passenger landaulet, suitable as taxi, at DM 7,900, and in two styles as convertibles. The two-door B style was listed at DM 8,500 and the four-door D convertible at DM 9,500. (The six-passenger models were also listed as seven-passenger cars in other sales literature by the factory.) All models were quite generously equipped with usually extra cost optional features.

To emphasize the tremendous *Betriebswirtschaftlichkeit*—thriftiness of operation—the sales literature for the 260D showed graphically that a trip from Berlin to Paris, by way of Munich, Milano and Geneva with the diesel automobile equalled that from Berlin in the most direct way, via Hannover and Cologne, with a gasoline-engined car.

This indicated a saving of 38 percent in fuel. But since the actual cost of diesel fuel was considerably less than that of gasoline, the real saving was about 55 percent. Thus, while the gasoline-powered car would travel the 1,000-kilometer route to Paris from Berlin, the driver of a diesel-engined car, with the same displacement power unit, could travel

Original working drawing of the OM138 diesel engine

46

The 260D sedan of 1936

the longer 2,095 kilometer distance by way of Milano, Italy, and Geneva, Switzerland, to Paris, for the same fuel cost.

Although the general opinion of this new development in power for a passenger car was quite enthusiastic acceptance, the dominating negative aspect was the higher initial cost of the automobile. It was calculated that only after driving 100,000 kilometers could the original purchase price be equalized with the gasoline-powered car, and the *Allgemeine Automobil Zeitung,* issue 8 of 1936, stated "only as a taxicab could one recoup the additional expense in one and a half years of operation by the lower cost of fuel consumed."

However, mainly meant for commercial use, in actual practice the 260D had many ardent followers in the passenger car class. A striking instance of the remarkable durability was the experience with the vehicle owned by a transport company in Württemberg. Before this car was scrapped after thirteen years of use, it had covered 1,300,000 kilometers (811,330 miles). The engine was replaced after each 250,000 kilometers (156,025 miles), and the rear axle after 600,000 kilometers (374,460 miles). During the war it was used, or rather misused, to pull a heavy trailer for transporting cattle.

Map, illustrating distances traveled with gasoline- and diesel-engined cars

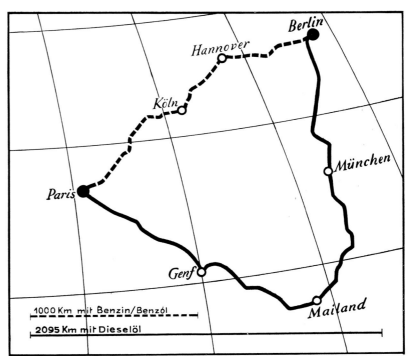

1000 Km mit Benzin/Benzöl ------

2095 Km mit Dieselöl

Technical Data

260D	
Engine type	4 cyl diesel (OM 138)
Bore and stroke	90 x 100mm (3.54 x 3.94 in)
Displacement	2545ccm (for tax purposes — 2527 ccm)
Engine speed at 95 km/hr	3000 rpm
Output	45 hp DIN
Firing order	1, 3, 4, 2
Wheelbase	3050mm (120 in)
Track, front and rear	1370/1390mm
Length	4800mm (189 in)
Height	1600mm (63 in)
Width	1710mm (67.3 in)
Ground clearance	200mm (8.7 in)
Weight of chassis	about 1100 kg (2420 lbs)
Weight of vehicle	about 1600 kg (3520 lbs)
Rear axle ratio	4.03:1
Turning circle	5.9 meters
Maximum speed, timed	95 km/hr (59.3 mph)
Maximum speed, approx.	100 km/hr (62.4 mph)
Fuel consumption	9–11 liters (about 24 mpg)
Oil consumption	0.25 liters
Fuel tank capacity	50 liters (13.2 gal)
Reserve of above	4 liters
Climbing rate, 1st gear	28%
2nd gear	20%
3rd gear	9%
4th gear	5%
Battery capacity	105 amp/hrs
Battery power	12 volt
Cooling system	11 liters
Oil capacity	5 liters
Tires	5.5 x 17 balloon

Some difficulties were reported by owners of the taxis in northern Germany when, during the bitter cold winter mornings at way below the freezing point temperatures, their engines would not start. Usually the paraffin in the diesel fuel had solidified in the long, thin fuel lines from the tank to the engine.

Because of its sturdy construction, the 260D model needed little attention (and the absense of sparkplugs, distributor, and carburetor made for considerable less service expense), the vehicle was most reasonable to operate. Until the beginning of World War II over 20,000 units of this model were produced by the factory. Many of them were driven as much as a million miles, according to a survey made.

The 2.6-liter diesel engine was improved to develop 50 horsepower in the summer of 1939, but only a few months later the war interferred with this work and no model change was made. Ill-informed critics will occasionally doubt that the Mercedes-Benz 260D was the first production diesel-engine passenger car manufactured. At the 1936 Berlin Auto Show, where the 260D was first introduced, the Hanomag Company exhibited a diesel-engined passenger car. This 1.9-liter displacement unit developed 35 horsepower at 3,000 revolutions per minute. Although created in November 1935, no complete cars were available to customers until 1938. The diesel engine was placed in a Rekord model, originally built in 1935 for the 1.5-liter gasoline power unit. In 1939, engineer Haeberle drove a car with a somewhat further developed—to 4,000 revolutions per minute—engine on the autobahn near Dessau to a record of 86.9 kilometers (54.23 miles) per hour for the standing start and 156.0 kilometers (97.36 miles) per hour for the flying start. Until 1940 a total of 2,572 diesel-engined Hanomag models were sold.

Production of the 260D [138] (from January 1936 to September 1939) was over 20,000 units

Model 170D

After the devastation of the manufacturing facilities, with the Untertürkheim plant 75 percent destroyed and the Sindelfingen assembly plant an almost total loss, the rubble was cleared away and production of vehicles was resumed in June 1946. In addition to the L3500 light trucks, the former smaller passenger car model was also again produced. The body and engine for the 170 sedan, first introduced in 1936, remained unchanged.

Director Max Wagner, who headed the construction work during 1945 to 1948, had urged the further development of the smaller dieselengined passenger model, and later, along with the gasoline engines for the 170V model, a diesel engine, also displacing 1.7 liters, was produced and installed in the same W136 chassis, called the 170D. In this design special stress was placed on economy, then a highly desired item by most automobile owners.

The four-cylinder diesel-engined car was first introduced to the public on May 20, 1949, at the *Export-Messe* at Hannover. It had undergone comprehensive testing in 1948, but pre-production was only begun in May 1949, with regular series production starting in July. (Until October 1953 a total of 33,823 units of all the D models, a and b, were built.) The price was DM 9,200.

The experience gained from the 2.6-liter diesel engine for passenger cars in 1936 was used to best advantage by Fritz Nallinger in the development of this smaller OM 636/I diesel engine. It used the same pre-combustion chamber system which had proved quite satisfactory before. With a bore of 73.5 millimeters (2.98 inches) and stroke of 100 millimeters (3.94 inches), it displaced 1,697 cubic centimeters (103.5 cubic inches) and developed 38 horsepower (DIN) at 3,200 revolutions per minute. Compression ratio was 19 to 1. The torque curve of 9.8 meters/kilogram, or 70.9 pounds/feet, at 2,000 revolutions per minute was very strong over a wide range of engine speeds.

This diesel engine had the liveliness and other desirable qualities of a gasoline engine, and indeed, in many respects, it was even better than that four-cylinder engine which had exactly the same specifications and provided the very same horsepower output.

The 170D sedan of 1949

**Fritz Nallinger,
Chief Engineer,
1935-1963**

49

The 170D sedan of 1950

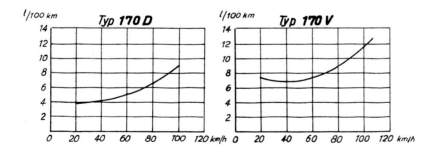

Fuel comparison chart with gasoline engine

The four-door 170 sedans had the pre-war, slightly slanted pointed radiators. The X-shaped frame was of oval steel tubing, and the suspension was the independent Mercedes-Benz type, first used in 1931 in their racing cars. It was used in all subsequent models.

Those who were prejudiced against the diesel automobile because of the usual annoying rattling and knocking when the engine was cold or idling, and objected to the odor of the fuel, could not help admitting that this criticism paled when considering the many valuable and truly fantastic advantages which this car possessed. Actually, this 1.7-liter four-cylinder diesel engine exceeded all standards of economy in operation, efficiency, quietness, dependability, temperament, and simplicity of service that was heretofore known of a diesel engine for a vehicle of any kind.

Difficult starting in cold weather was solved by necessitating a longer glowplug period. The lower cost of fuel and considerably better mileage than that of a gasoline-powered automobile, lower maintenance and service costs were of no small significance to the owners. Fuel consumption was calculated at 6.5 to 7 liters per 100 kilometers (62.4 miles), but the 7.5 liter figure sometimes quoted seemed more accurate. That would be 32 miles per gallon. The 170V model used 11 liters (21 miles per gallon). Oil consumption was 0.10 liters per 100 kilometers.

A sales brochure of the time features a *"Weltrekord der Wirtschaftlichkeit"*—World-record of Economy— when a factory sponsored 170D sedan on a test drive from Stuttgart to Hamburg, a distance of 698 kilometers (436 miles) used 45 liters of fuel oil. That sparse consumption rated a 6.5 liters per kilometers, or 36 miles per gallon, average. (An interesting sidelight is the fact that when many years before, the People's Car, the Volkswagen, was designed as the very ideal vehicle, the formula was to achieve 100 kilometers per 100 kilogram on one liter of fuel (gasoline). The 170D weighed 1,250, and used just half that amount!)

A slightly improved version, the 170Da, was produced from June 1950 until May 1952. The OM 636 engine developed 40 horsepower at 3,200 revolutions per minute and the car had a maximum speed of 100 kilometers (62.4 miles) per hour. This was also its cruising speed, and the factory literature suggested that it could be maintained for the longest periods, continuously. Fuel consumption was still improved over the older model, and now the average use was 6.4 liters per 100

Upper left: the 170Db sedan of 1952.
Right: the 170SD sedan of 1953. Upper
right: steering wheel and instrument panel
of 170DS.

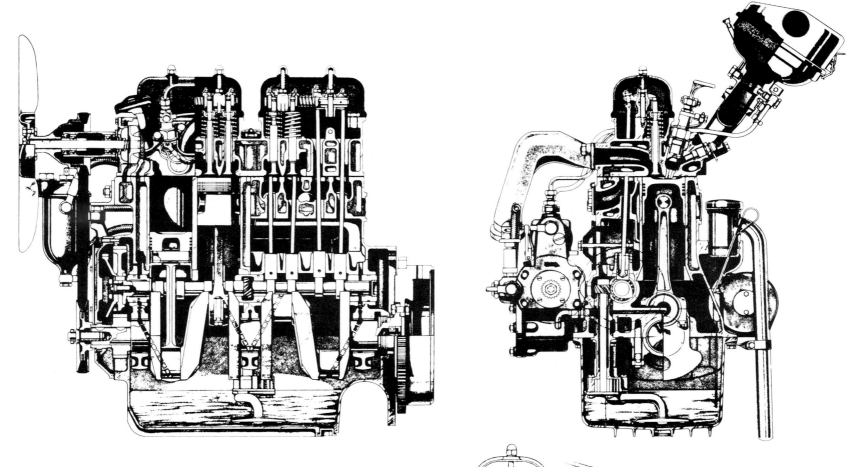

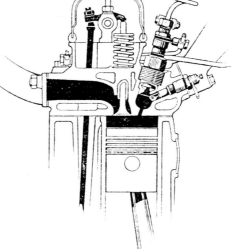

Above: longitudinal section of the OM636 diesel engine for the 170D model. *Upper right:* cross section of the OM636 diesel engine for the 170D. *Right:* pre-chamber injection arrangement of the diesel engine.

kilometers of driving. That equaled, in cost, a gasoline consumption of a mere 3.8 gallons, unattainable, of course, in any automobile of that day.

Journalists were enthused over this new model and Paul Schweder wrote in the ADAC magazine, number 11/1950, that he "reached 109 kilometers when testing the 170Da on a 400-kilometer drive on the autobahn." He averaged 95 kilometers (56.3 miles) per hour. "This automobile demonstrated perhaps the greatest motorized advance of 1950." And Richard Gebauer, writing in the NKZ, number 16/1950, stated that never had he found it so difficult to relinquish a test car, as the 170Da. The car belonged, because of its driving characteristics, performance, and equipment to the *Spitzengruppe* (top group) of German passenger cars.

The price of the 170Da four-door sedan was initially DM 8,620, but on March 31, 1951, rose to DM 9,390. (To ease the shock of a price rise, it was listed at DM 8,900 without tires.) They were listed at DM 490, for five. Optional extras were (from 1950) a Becker radio and (from 1951) the sunroof.

The 170Da was also available as an ambulance. Built by the Lueg factory at Bochum, the Daimler-Benz chassis was furnished from June 1950 until February 1952. The vehicle weighed 1,440 kilograms and sold for DM 10,990 at first, but eventually for DM 11,950. (With tires!)

The 170Db was the next version of this line and production started in May 1952 when the former model was phased out. Actually, there was no great difference in these models, except that the row of vertical louvers on the sides of the engine compartment were eliminated for two long horizontal slits below chrome strips. Engine specifications of the OM636 remained exactly as before, but fuel consumption was now given as 6.1 liters per 100 kilometers and attention was called to the fact that the diesel engine was actually more economical when the vehicle was fully loaded—in contrast to the performance of a gasoline engine.

The 170Db sold for DM 8,950 and was built until March 19, 1954. All of these three versions had the W136 body style, and total production of this line was 33,823 units. Yearly production was, from 1949 on, 907 units, 5,609 units, 14,622 units, 8,115 units, and 4,570 units for the last year, 1953.

The 170DS model was considered a new line entirely. Sharing the body with the 170S gasoline-engined car which had a new, more powerful engine of 52 horsepower, the diesel version kept the previous power unit. And all technical details remained as well. Maximum speed was the same, and the 6.1-liter fuel consumption was as economical as before and was always prominently mentioned in all literature on the car. First built in January 1952, a total of 12,985 units were manufactured until August 1953. The price was DM 10,800, with an optional heater for DM 185.

The refined 170S-D model was introduced in September 1953 by Fritz Nallinger. It was based on the previous 170Db type, which in turn shared its basic design with the 170S model, the gasoline-powered version of the same passenger sedan.

The four-cylinder OM 636 diesel engine had the unchanged bore of 75 millimeters and stroke of 100 millimeters, displacing 1,767 cubic centimeters (107.7 cubic inches), and developed 40 horsepower at 3,200 revolutions per minute. The compression ratio was 19 to 1. Firing order of the cylinders was 1-3-4-2. Electrically heated glow plugs in the cylinder heads, which could be controlled by means of a turn button on the dashboard, made certain the starting of the engine in even the coldest winter temperatures within a few seconds with absolute assurance. A circulating pump, driven by the engine, ascertained quick cooling water circulation and the thermostat provided for the automatic constant of proper and uniform operating temperature.

The wheelbase of the sedan was still 2,845 millimeters (112 inches), but the wider track was, in the front 1,310 millimeters (51.57 inches) and in the rear 1,435 millimeters (56.49 inches), improving the road holding qualities of the car still futher. The overall length of the 170SD was 4,450 millimeters (175.19 inches), maximum width 1,685 millimeters (62.98 inches), and body height 1,590 millimeters (62.59 inches). Ground clearance was 185 millimeters (7.28 inches). The total weight of the car was 1,280 kilograms (2,816 pounds), the chassis alone weighing 850 kilograms (1,870 pounds). Tires fitted were 5.50×16, and the turning circle was about 12 meters (39.37 feet).

Only the front axle assembly was actually the same as that of the earlier model. All other components had been slightly altered in this new series. The body remained the same, although interior space was increased by 8.7 percent. New front leaf springs and coils in the rear had greater specific elasticity, and the front and rear telescopic shock absorbers were adapted to the new softer springing and weight distribution.

Drawing of the chassis

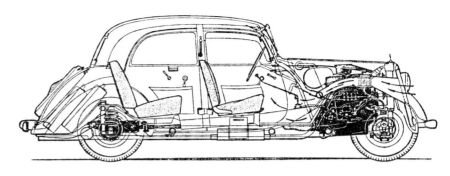

Drawing of the 170D body

Maximum speed was still calculated as 100 kilometers (62 miles) per hour and suggested continuous cruising speed was the same. The quiet running of the engine was assured by the careful balancing and enclosing of all moving parts as well as the placing of the entire power unit on heavy soft-rubber cushions in such a manner that, especially at high speeds, hardly a difference could be noted between this and a gasoline engine.

The enlarged fuel tank held 47 liters (12.4 U.S. gallons) thus extending the driving range to 600-700 kilometers (370-470 miles), or the distance from Hamburg to Munich—at a fuel cost of DM 19. The crankcase had a capacity of maximum of 4 liters (1.32 gallons) and minimum of 2.5 liters (0.64 gallons).

Climbing ability of the car was in first gear 33 percent, in second 17 percent, in third 9 percent, and in fourth gear 6 percent. The maximum allowable speed in the gears was 26.5 kilometers (16.42 miles) per hour in first, 47 kilometers (29.21 miles) in second, 75 kilometers (46.6 miles) in third, and about 100 kilometers (62.41 miles) in fourth gear.

The battery was 2×6 volt V/84 ampere hours. The capacity of the cooling system was 9 liters (2.37 gallons) without heating, and 10.1 liters (2.7 gallons) with the Daimler-Benz heating installation.

The price of the improved model was actually over 15 percent less than that of the previous one, DM 9,350 against DM 10,985 for the DS model. And by February 1954, the price was actually reduced to DM 8,900,

including the heater. Until September 1955, a total of 14,887 units were manufactured.

As before, an ambulance, built by the Lueg factory at Bochum, was made available. This vehicle was constructed from December 1953 until November 1954, and a total of 121 units were sold. The price was DM 12,750 in January 1954 and was reduced a month later, actually on February 22, to DM 12,500, including the heating unit.

Production of the 170D, 170Da, and 170Db [136 I-VI] (from May 1949 to October 1953)

was in	1949	907 units
	1950	5,609 units
	1951	14,622 units
	1952	8,115 units
	1953	4,570 units
	total	33,823 units

Production of the 170DS [191] (from January 1952 until August 1953)

was in	1952	6,734 units
	1953	6,251 units
	total	12,985 units

Production of the 170 S-D [136 VIII] (from July 1953 until September 1955)

was in	1953	6,494 units
	1954	5,992 units
	1955	2,401 units
	total	14,887 units

Technical Data

	170D *(W136)*	170Da / 170Db *(W136)*	170DS *(W191)*	170S-D *(W136)*
Engine type	4 cyl diesel (OM 636)	4 cyl diesel (OM 636 IV & VI)	4 cyl diesel (OM 636 VI)	4 cyl diesel (OM 636 VI)
Bore and stroke	73.5 x 100mm (2.98 x 3.94 in)	75 x 100mm (2.95 x 3.94 in)	75 x 100mm (2.95 x 3.94 in)	75 x 100mm (2.95 x 3.94 in)
Displacement	1697 cc (103.5 cu in)	1767 cc (107.7 cu in)	1767 cc (107.7 cu in)	1767 cc (107.7 cu in)
Power output	38 hp (DIN) @ 3200 rpm	40 hp (DIN) @ 3200 rpm	40 hp (DIN) @ 3200 rpm	40 hp (DIN) @ 3200 rpm
Compression ratio	19:1	19:1	19:1	19:1
Torque	9.8 mkg @ 2000 rpm (70.9 ft/lb)	9.8 mkg @ 2000 rpm (70.9 ft/lb)	10.3 mkg @ 2000 rpm (74.5 ft/lb)	10.3 mkg @ 2000 rpm (74.5 ft/lb)
Carburetion	Bosch injection pump (pre-combustion chamber)		Bosch injection pump (pre-combustion chamber)	
Engine speed at 100 km/hr	3330 rpm	3330 rpm	3330 rpm	3330 rpm
Gear ratios	I. 4.025:1 II. 2.280:1 III. 1.420:1 IV. 1.000:1	I. 4.025:1 II. 2.280:1 III. 1.420:1 IV. 1.000:1	I. 4.025:1 II. 2.280:1 III. 1.420:1 IV. 1.000:1	I. 4.025:1 II. 2.280:1 III. 1.420:1 IV. 1.000:1
Rear axle ratio	4.125:1	4.125:1	4.125:1	4.125:1
Chassis	X-shaped oval tubular	X-shaped oval tubular	X-shaped oval tubular	X-shaped oval tubular
Suspension	independent front and rear swing axle with coil springs		independent front and rear swing axle with coil springs	
Brakes and area	drum, 564 cm² (87.4 sq in)	drum, 736 cm² (114 sq in)	drum, 736 cm² (114 sq in)	drum, 736 cm² (114 sq in)
Wheelbase	2845mm (112 in)	2845mm (112 in)	2845mm (112 in)	2845mm (112 in)
Track, front/rear	1310/1296mm (51.6/51.0in)	Da: 1310/1342mm (51.6/52.8 in) Db: 1310/1360mm (51.6/53.5 in)	1310/1435mm (51.6/56.5 in)	1310/1435mm (51.6/56.5 in)
Length	4285mm (168.7 in)	4285mm (168.7 in)	4455mm (175.4 in)	4450mm (175.2 in)
Width	1580mm (62.2 in)	1630mm (64.2 in)	1684mm (66.3 in)	1685mm (66.3 in)
Height	1610mm (63.4 in)	1610mm (63.4 in)	1610mm (63.4 in)	1590mm (62.6 in)
Ground clearance	185mm (7.3 in)	185mm (7.3 in)	185mm (7.3 in)	185mm (7.3 in)
Tires	5.50 x 16	5.50 x 16	5.50 x 16	5.50 x 16
Turning circle	11.5 meters (37.7 ft)	11.5 meters (37.7 ft)	12 meters (39.37 ft)	12 meters (39.37 ft)
Steering type and ratio	worm, 14.4:1	worm, 14.4:1	worm, 13.9:1	worm, 14.1:1
Weight	1250 kg (2750 lbs)	1250 kg (2750 lbs)	1275 kg (2805 lbs)	1300 kg (2860 lbs)
Maximum speed	100 km/hr (62 mph)	105 km/hr (65 mph)	105 km/hr (65 mph)	105 km/hr (65 mph)
Acceleration	58 sec 0-100 km	50 sec 0-100 km	56 sec 0-100 km	56 sec 0-100 km
Fuel consumption	7.5 liters/100 km (32 mpg)	7.5 liters/100 km (32 mpg)	8.5 liters/100 km (27.75 mpg)	8.5 liters/100 km (27.75 mpg)
Fuel tank capacity	37 liters (9.8 gallons)	37 liters (9.8 gallons)	47 liters (12.4 gallons)	47 liters (12.4 gallons)

The 180D sedan of 1953

Model 180D

The new 180D model—W120—was introduced in the late fall of 1953 and regular production began in February 1954. Earlier a radically new type of chassis—the frame-floor unit with a sub frame—had been developed for the 180 sedan and now the diesel-engined version of that line became available.

The *Rahmenbodenanlage* (frame floor assembly) represented an entirely new idea, although the former X-shaped oval steel tube frame which had been used on the 170, 220, and 300 line of cars had proved quite satisfactory. The most important elements of this new design—the high sectional steel tubes—were solidly united to the floor of the body to form a platform that was especially resistant to distortion. This actually doubled the assembly's rigidity and lessened noise most considerably. The sub frame which carried the complete power unit and transmission, as well as the steering and the front wheel assembly, was anchored to the front part of the main chassis on rubber blocks on the three-point suspension system. This arrangement offered advantages both in manufacture and maintenance. It was, too, the first example of a design where heavy components were readily detachable.

The new 180D model had a wheelbase of 2,650 millimeters (104.3 inches), front track of 1,430 millimeters (56.3 inches) and rear of 1,475 millimeters (58.1 inches). The overall length of the car was 4,485 millimeters (176.6 inches) and width was 1,740 millimeters (68.5 inches). Ground clearance was 185 millimeters (7.3 inches) and the turning circle was 11.5 meters (38 feet). The tires fitted were 6.40×13. The fuel tank held 56 liters (14.8 gallons).

The early 180D model was fitted with the slightly enlarged new OM 636 VII engine which still developed 40 horsepower at 3,200 revolutions per minute. But the new maximum speed was given as 112 kilometers (70 miles) per hour, a slight increase over the former performance. Fuel consumption was 8 liters per 100 kilometers, actually less than 2.5 gallons of diesel oil per 100 miles of driving, or nearly 30 miles per gallon. (The gasoline four-cylinder side-valve engine of the 180 model developed 52 horsepower at 4,000 revolutions per minute.)

An improved diesel engine was introduced in September 1955. The overhead valve diesel engine now developed 43 horsepower at

The innovative frame-floor assembly of the 180D

Sub-frame with engine, gear box, front axle and steering assembly; Drive shaft; Single-joint swing axle, suspension; Diagram of single-joint swing axle

Above: The OM636 VII diesel engine of the 180D.
Below: The 180D sedan of 1955.

3,500 revolutions per minute. This improved the performance of the popular and highly economical automobile—the maximum and cruising speed was 115 kilometers (72 miles) per hour—of which over 30,000 units were produced by the end of 1955.

With the introduction of German automobiles in the United States a rather confusing horsepower rating was also introduced. The official American rating of the American Engineers Standard (SAE) is about 10 percent higher than the official rating of the corresponding Deutsche Ingenieur Norm (DIN) rating. Thus, many times different horsepower output figures are given for the same engine, causing great anguish to the serious automotive writer and immense bewilderment to the conscientious reader. The 43 (DIN) horsepower of the 180D engine, for instance, became 46 (SAE) in the U.S.

The price of the 180D was $3,394 in the United States. A total of 116,485 units of the 180D were built from 1953 to 1959.

To illustrate the dependability of the diesel automobile, it was decided to participate in the strenuous Mille Miglia in 1955. Three 180D models won the first three places in their Special diesel class, averaging over 60 miles per hour for the 922 mile-long race through Italy. And on February 14-17, 1959 a 180D won in its class at the Garmisch-Partenkirchen Rallye in miserable weather.

The 180Db model was produced from July 1959 until August 1961. The car had a larger diameter brakes, a wider radiator shell and no bumper overriders. The single swing axle had already first appeared on the older model in September 1955, as had the window wings. A total of 24, 676 units of the 180Db were built.

The 180Dc, manufactured from June 1961 until October 1962, had the enlarged OM 621 IV diesel engine of 1,988 cubic centimeters (121.3 cubic inches) and 48 horsepower at 3,800 revolutions per minute. At that time a 55 horsepower diesel engine at 4,200 revolutions per minute was also installed in the 190Dc model which will be described in detail later. The 190D model had already been in production for four years, but with a somewhat less powerful engine (of 50 horsepower).

Performance of the 180Dc was, of course, improved by this change—torque was up to 11 meters/kilogram from 10.3—and the acceleration improved from 39 to 36 seconds for the 0-100 kilometers speed. Maximum speed was 120 kilometers (75 miles) per hour, although the 180D model, after September 1955, did 115 instead of the original 112 kilometers (70 miles) per hour.

A 180D at the Mille Miglia, 1955

At a check point at the Mille Miglia, 1955

The 180D four-door sedan sold in 1954 for DM 10,300, but was steadily reduced until in 1958-1961 it sold for DM 9,200. The 180Dc, however, sold for DM 9,850 in 1962.

The 180Dc production in the two years totaled 11,822 units. Of all of the 180D models, a total of 152,983 units were built in the ten years.

Production of the 180D model [120 I] (from October 1953/February 1954 until July 1959)

	was in	1953	11 units
		1954	15,532 units
		1955	20,345 units
		1956	21,013 units
		1957	22,910 units
		1958	26,693 units
		1959	9,981 units
		total	116,485 units

Production of the 180Db [120 II] (from July 1959 until August 1961)

	was in	1959	8,076 units
		1960	11,151 units
		1961	5,449 units
		total	24,676 units

Production of the 180Dc [120 III] (from June 1961 until October 1962)

	was in	1961	4,822 units
		1962	7,000 units
		total	11,822 units

Winner of the 1957 International Winter-Rallye Garmisch-Partenkirchen

The 180D sedan of 1961-1962

Technical Data

	180D / 180Db *(W120)*	180Dc *(W120)*
Engine type	4 cyl diesel (OM 636 VII)	4 cyl diesel (OM 621 IV)
Bore and stroke	75 x 100mm (2.96 x 3.94 in)	87 x 83.6mm (3.43 x 3.29 in)
Displacement	1767 cc (107.7 cu in)	1988 cc (121 cu in)
Power output	40 hp (DIN) @ 3200 rpm 46 hp (SAE) @ 3500 rpm from Sept. '55: 43 hp @ 3500	48 hp (DIN) @ 3800 rpm
Compression ratio	19:1	21:1
Torque	10.3mgk @2000 rpm (75ft/lb)	11mkg @2200rpm (80ft/lb)
Fuel injection	Bosch injection pump (pre-combustion chamber)	
Engine speed at 100 km/hr	3220 rpm	3350 rpm
Gear ratios	I. 4.05:1 (15.0) II. 2.38:1 (8.81) III. 1.53:1 (5.66) IV. 1.00:1 (3.70)	I. 4.05:1 (15.0) II. 2.38:1 (8.81) III. 1.53:1 (5.66) IV. 1.00:1 (3.70)
Rear axle ratio	3.70 (37:10)	3.70 (37:10)
Chassis	unit frame and body	unit frame and body
Suspension	independent front, swing axle rear, with coil springs from Sept. '55: single swing axle	rear: single swing axle
Brakes and area	drum, 816 cm² (126.5 sq in)	drum, 1064 cm² (164.9 sq in)
Wheelbase	2650mm (104.3 in)	2650mm (104.3 in)
Track, front/rear	1430/1475mm (56.3/58.1 in)	1430/1475mm (56.3/58.1 in)
Length	4485mm (176.6 in)	4485mm (176.6 in)
Width	1740mm (68.5 in)	1740mm (68.5 in)
Height	1560mm (61.4 in)	1560mm (61.4 in)
Ground clearance	185mm (7.3 in)	185mm (7.3 in)
Tires	6.40 x 13	6.40 x 13
Turning circle	11.5 meters (38 ft)	11.5 meters (38 ft)
Steering type and ratio	recirculating ball, 18.5:1	recirculating ball, 18.5:1
Weight	1220 kg (2684 lbs)	1220 kg (2684 lbs)
Maximum speed	112 km/hr (70 mph) from Sept. '55: 115 km/hr	120 km/hr (75 mph)
Acceleration	39 sec 0-100 km from Sept. '55: 37 sec	36 sec 0-100 km
Fuel consumption	8 liters/100 km (29.3 mpg)	8 liters/100 km (29.3 mpg)
Fuel tank capacity	56 liters (14.8 gallons)	56 liters (14.8 gallons)

Karl Kling and 190D at a rest stop along the route

Mediterranée-Le Cap Rallye

Again, to emphasize the fantastic dependability and economy of their diesel passenger cars, Daimler-Benz decided to enter what was then perhaps the most difficult test for any car, the African Rallye *Mediterranée-Le Cap*.

It was the first participation of the company and the drivers, Karl Kling with Rainer Günzler. The 190D was basically a production model.

A total of 28 vehicles started on their excruciating journey in February 1959 from the harbor at Alger, Algiers. Kling took the lead immediately—and kept it. The competition included Citroen ID19, Land Rover, Volkswagen, Simca, and others. The cars drove in daily stages of from 400 to 1,000 kilometers with two most demanding special trials on the way.

The tortuous route led from Algiers on the Mediterranean through the blowing dusty sands of the Sahara desert and the steaming jungles of Nigeria to Kano. Then the cars drove past Lake Chad and Fort Lamy, down into Central Africa and the vast expanses of the Congo with its thick equatorial forests and wide rivers. At Stanleyville the route turned east from sweltering heat onto higher ground toward the cooler mountains, then south through thick brush country past Lake Tanganyika into Elizabethville, still in the torrid Congo. Lusaka, Rodesia, and Livingston were next, and the spectacular Victoria Falls in Nyasaland were barely touched. Then came more difficult driving into Bulawaga and across more streams to Pretoria and finally Cape Town, South Africa, at the Cape of Good Hope.

It was an exhausting trip from the dry desert lands through steppe, tropical woodland and savanna, rain forests and mountains and wide plains and any sort of terrain imaginable.

The victorious drivers, Karl Kling and his assistant Rainer Günzler, had accumulated 191 points, without any penalties on the 14,045 kilometer (8,727.15 mile) long drive. Their speed was a fantastic 80.6 kilometer (50.5 mile) per hour average, especially when considering that the former record was 65 kilometers per hour.

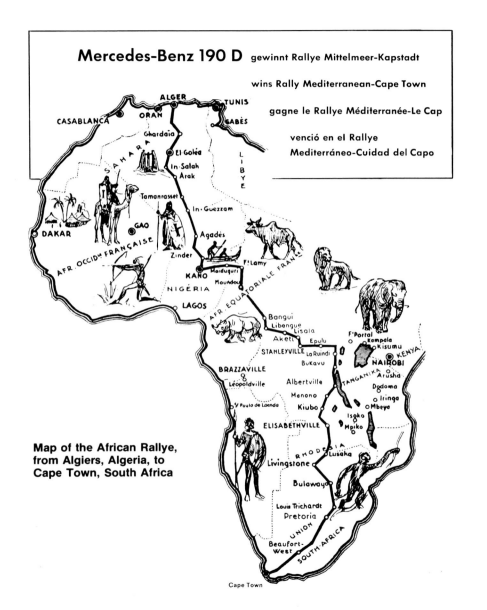

Mercedes-Benz 190 D gewinnt Rallye Mittelmeer-Kapstadt

wins Rally Mediterranean-Cape Town

gagne le Rallye Méditerranée-Le Cap

venció en el Rallye Mediterráneo-Cuidad del Capo

Map of the African Rallye, from Algiers, Algeria, to Cape Town, South Africa

After the rallye, Kling stated that he was completely convinced that a production diesel passenger car could cross the Dark Continent—and especially the Congo with the nearly impenetrable jungle paths—without great difficulties, but perhaps at a slower pace than he. Kling rated the 190D very highly because the car needed no repairs on the way and not even a tire change.

The victory in the Fourth Africa-Rallye was indeed a remarkable achievement for car and drivers, and proved again the excellent qualities of a diesel-engined Mercedes-Benz.

Above: **Kling's 190D at the entrance to a settlement in the Congo.**
Below: **Crowds of natives line the roads to watch the competitors**

MERCEDES - BENZ

ALGIERS - CAPE RALLY 1959

Upper left: A relaxed Kling after a long and strenuous drive through Africa. *Upper right:* Victor Karl Kling with Rainer Günzler in Cape Town. *Left:* Kling cleaning radiator of bugs before posing for photographers.

The 190D sedan of 1958-1961

Model 190D

The 190D model—W121—was first introduced in August 1958, fully two years after the gasoline version. The diesel engine, enlarged to displace 1,897 cubic centimeters (115.7 cubic inches), and placed in a newly styled and more elegant looking body, developed 50 DIN, or 55 SAE, horsepower at 4,000 revolutions per minute. It was a larger and more powerful addition to the still available 180D, which remained in the older style body. That model still had the 43 horsepower engine until 1961.

The 190D was by 30 kilograms a slightly heavier car, but the acceleration of 0 to 100 kilometers per hour was better by 8 seconds, and the maximum speed, which was also the cruising speed, at 126 kilometers (78 miles) per hour, was better by 14 kilometers. And the fuel consumption of this larger model was only 0.5 liters more per 100 kilometers of driving.

The 190Db had a wider radiator and wider bumpers without overriders, as did the 180Db model, but the engine remained the same as before. The 190D sedan sold in 1958 for DM 9,950, and it sold for $3,768 in the United States.

The 190D outsold the 180D model from its introduction by a wide margin. From 1959 on until 1961, when both diesel automobiles were the b types, the 190Db sold 61,309 units, while the less powerful 180Db sold only 24,676 units.

The 190Dc model was produced from June 1961 until August 1965. The OM 621 III overhead camshaft diesel engine with a bore of 87 millimeters (3.43 inches) and stroke of 83.6 millimeters (3.29 inches) displaced 1,988 cubic centimeters (121.3 cubic inches) and developed 55 DIN, or 60 SAE, horsepower at 4,200 revolutions per minute. (Maximum engine speed allowed was 4,300 revolutions.) It was equipped with a four-plunger pump with injection timer, made by Robert Bosch. Compression ratio was 21 to 1. Torque or 87 feet/pounds at 2,400 revolutions per minute gave it remarkable acceleration power.

The all-synchronized Daimler-Benz four-speed gear box was controlled by the gear shift lever mounted on the steering column. An automatic transmission was also available, the first time on a diesel-engined automobile. The frame was of the frame-floor unit construction

Above: Front view of the 190D. **Below:** Rear view of the 190D.

Left: Instrument panel of the 190D. *Below:* Interior appointments of the 190D, 1958-1961.

Above: **The 190D sedan of 1961.**
Below: **The OM621 diesel engine of the 190D, 1958.**

welded to a semi-supporting body. The body style was that of the new 220 series with the slight suggestion of rear fins, except that the hood was slightly shorter. The new style was larger, longer, and lower. It did not have the same headlight treatment of the six-cylinder line of cars, but had round lights and a simpler bumper, without guards. The wheelbase was slightly less (2,700 millimeters, or 106.3 inches). The overall weight of the car was 1,320 kilograms (2,904 pounds). The rear axle was the famed Daimler-Benz single-joint swing axle with low pivot point. Two-circuit hydraulic booster brakes were provided. In front were disc brakes, in the rear drum brakes with turbo cooling. The rear axle ratio was 3.92 to 1. The maximum speed of 130 kilometers (81 miles) with manual transmission and 127 kilometers (79 miles) per hour with automatic, was also the suggested cruising speed of the car— the usual practice. The electric system was operated by the 66 ampere/hours battery at 12 volts. Fuel consumption with the manual transmission was 9 liters per 100 kilometers (26 miles per gallon) and 10 liters (23.5 miles per gallon) with the automatic transmission.

The 190Dc four-door sedan sold in 1961 for DM 10,450, and the price of the 190Dc was $4,000 in the United States. From 1961 until August 1965 a total of 225,645 units of the 190Dc model were produced.

On April 8, 1965, the flower-covered 500,000th diesel passenger automobile came off the assembly line in the Sindelfingen plant amidst great jubilation of the huge crowd of workers and company officials who had come to celebrate this historic event.

Production of the 190D model [121 I] (from August 1958 until July 1959)

was in	1958	5,469 units
	1959	15,160 units
	total	20,629 units

Production of the 190Db [121 II] (from June 1959 until September 1961)

was in	1959	13,709 units
	1960	29,116 units
	1961	18,484 units
	total	61,309 units

Production of the 190Dc model [110] (from April/June 1961 until August 1965)

was in	1961	12,882 units
	1962	45,414 units
	1963	60,784 units
	1964	64,422 units
	1965	42,143 units
	total	225,645 units

Technical Data

	190D / 190Db *(W121)*	190Dc *(W110)*			
Engine type	4 cyl diesel, overhead camshaft (OM 621)	(OM 621 III)			
Bore and stroke	85 x 83.6mm (3.35 x 3.29 in)	87 x 83.6mm (3.43 x 3.29 in)			
Displacement	1897 cc (115.7 cu in)	1988 cc (121.27 cu in)			
Power output	50 hp (DIN) @ 4000 rpm (55 hp SAE)	55 hp (DIN) @ 4200 rpm (60 hp SAE)			
Compression ratio	21:1	21:1			
Torque	11mkg @2200 rpm(79.5 ft/lbs)	11.5 mkg 2400 rpm 12 mkg SAE 87 ft/lbs)			
Fuel injection	Bosch injection pump pre-combustion chamber	Bosch injection pump			
Engine speed at 100 km/hr	3220 rpm	3350 rpm			
Gear ratios	I. 4.05:1 II. 2.38:1 III. 1.53:1 IV. 1.00:1	I. 4.05:1 II. 2.28:1 III. 1.53:1 IV. 1.00:1	automatic	I. 3.98:1 II. 2.52:1 III. 1.58:1 IV. 1.00:1	
Rear axle ratio	3.70	3.92			
Chassis	unit frame and body	unit frame and body			
Suspension	independent front, single joint swing axle rear, with coil springs from 1963: air suspension, optional				
Brakes and area	drum, 1064 cm² (164.9 sq in)	drum, 1064 cm² (164.9 sq in) servo assisted from Aug. '63: disc, front			
Wheelbase	2650mm (104.3 in)	2700mm (106.3 in)			
Track, front/rear	1430/1475mm (56.2/58.1 in)	1468/1485mm (58/58.5 in) from Aug.'63: 1482/1485mm (58.3/58.5 in)			
Length	4485mm (176.6 in) b: 4500mm (177.2 in)	4730mm (186.5 in)			
Width	1740mm (68.5 in)	1795mm (70.7 in)			
Height	1560mm (61.4 in)	1495mm (58.8 in)			
Ground clearance	185mm (7.3 in)	185mm (7.3 in)			
Tires	6.40 x 13	7.00 x 13			
Turning circle	11.5 meters (38 ft)	11.8-11.6 meters (38 ft)			
Steering type and ratio	recirculating ball, 18.5:1 (3.75 turns)	recirculating ball, 21.4:1; from May '64: servo assisted 17.3:1 (3.2 turns)			
Weight	1250 kg (2750 lbs)	1320 kg (2904 lbs)			
Maximum speed	126 km/hr (78 mph)	130 km/hr (81 mph); automatic 127 km/hr (79 mph)			
Acceleration	29 sec 0-100 km	29 sec 0-100 km/hr; automatic 30 sec 0-100 km/hr			
Fuel consumption	8.5 liters/100 km (27.75 mpg)	9 liters/100 km (26 mpg); automatic 10 liters/100 km (23.5 mpg)			
Fuel tank capacity	56 liters (14.8 gallons)	52 liters (13.5 gallons)			

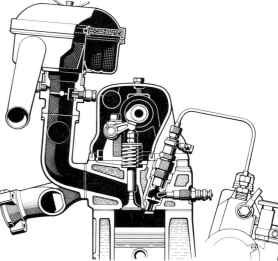

Drawing of the cylinder head of the OM621 engine

Model 200D

The 200D model—W110—was introduced at the Frankfurt Auto Show in 1965 (actually the 42nd *Internationale Automobil-Ausstellung*). That year, Daimler-Benz offered a total of 17 models of pasenger cars. This diesel-engined sedan, however, was practically the same car as before, except for the new horizontal rear light arrangement, turn indicators and parking lights below the headlights instead of in the fenders, and ventilator extractors on the rear roof pillars covered with chrome mouldings. The body was deeper by 20 millimeters for more comfortable seating. The OM 621 VIII engine displacement of the earlier model had, of course, been 2 liters (1,988 cubic centimeters) already. And, as before, it developed 55 DIN, or 60 SAE, horsepower at 4,200 revolutions per minute. The technical specifications were similar to those of the former engine, except for the newly designed five-bearing crankshaft and a number of other improvements which further increased the smoothness and quietness of the diesel engine. A new, three-section drive shaft was also installed for improved power transfer to the rear axle.

The maximum and cruising speed was therefore increased by 3 miles, to 81 miles per hour (130 kilometers) per hour, although the total weight of the sedan was increased by 5 kilograms to 2,915 pounds (1,325 kilograms). Overall length was 186.2 inches. Fuel consumption had consequently suffered and was slightly more than before, but still rather an economical 8.1 liters per 100 kilometers, or 29 miles per gallon, according to the DIN system. Other literature listed 9 liters (26 miles per gallon) and with automatic transmission 10 liters (23 miles per gallon) consumption for 100 kilometers. The automatic transmission, and the power steering, were optional extra items. the gearshift lever was on the steering column, but a floor shift was also available again.

A Daimler-Benz director stated that "this 200D model combined all of the qualities which have made the Mercedes-Benz diesel passenger cars so acceptable that over half a million such automobiles had been produced since 1936. Economy of operation, engine flexibility with rather lively performance, and robust construction—all giving long and reliable service with low maintenance costs—were skillfully combined in this model."

The 200D sedan of 1965

The price of the 200D model was DM 11,300 in Germany in 1965. In the United States it sold for $4,142. A year later, the prices had risen to DM 11,500 and $4,305, respectively. From July 1965 to February 1968 a total of 161,618 cars were produced.

In 1967 the 200D long became available. It had a 650 millimeters (25.59 inches) longer wheelbase, and was a 7 to 8 passenger limousine.

To stimulate interest in the diesel-engined passenger car program, Daimler-Benz arranged a unique rallye event in 1967. Five identical production 200D sedans, each carrying a journalist and

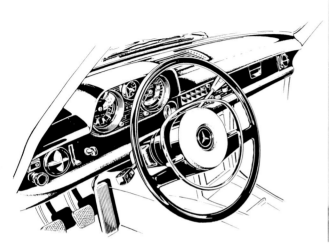

Upper left: Instrument panel drawing of the 200D, 1973. Below: The instrument panel of the 200D, 1965. Upper right: The 200D sedan of 1973.

neutral observer from an Auto Club as passengers, started from Stuttgart for different destinations. All would return to their starting places after two weeks of travel. The point of the exercise was to impress most graphically the prospective purchaser of a car that the actual travel radius of a diesel was 33 percent greater than that of a gasoline-engined vehicle. One full tank (65 liters) of fuel was sufficient for 720 kilometers (447 miles) of driving, against the 541 kilometers (336 miles) for the similar gasoline model. The places chosen were those a vacationer might select.

The drive to Istanbul, Turkey, and return, a trip of 5,134 kilometers, cost DM 159.65 for fuel, the Rovaniemi (Finland, on the Arctic Circle) trip of 6,234 kilometers cost DM 241.18, the Sicily, Italy, trip of 4,714 kilometers cost 234.05, the Lisbon, Portugal, trip of 6,012 kilometers cost DM 278.61, and the Moscow, Russia, trip of 6,576 kilometers cost DM 143.50.

The combined total distance of 440 hours of driving was 28,663 kilometers (17,810 miles), and 2,626 liters of fuel were used, averaging 9.16 liters (about 25 miles per gallon) per 100 kilometers. Driving at an average speed of 65 kilometers (slightly over 40 miles) per hour, the

actual cost per kilometer was 3.7 Pfennig. (The rate of exchange in 1967 was $3.98=DM 1.00. On that basis, it cost exactly 1.4726 cents per kilometer, or 2.369 cents per mile.) Economical traveling? Undisputedly. Troubles encountered? One flat tire.

Late in 1967 the New Generation body style—W115—was also made available for the 200D model. Nearly identical to the 250S body of 1966, but with many improvements, it had a considerably more elegant look, had a lower silhouette, lower center of gravity and wider radiator design than the previous type. And the rear fins were gone!

The OM 615 engine remained basically the same as before. The gear ratios were changed and for the United States market the rear axle ratio was 4.08:1 instead of the 3.92 elsewhere. Weight and maximum speed were practically the same as the older model—which sold 68,399 units in 1967.

From October 1967 unitl December 1976 a total of 339,927 units of the 200D model were built. It sold in 1968 for DM 12,000, which rose by 1975 to DM 17,185. In the United States the price was at first $4,494, but by 1970 it was $5,324.

When a new body style, the W123, was created for the middle class of cars, first introduced at the Geneva Auto Show (the *Salon de l'Auto Genève*) in March 1976, the 200D was one of the models with that body. Many new engineering features and high technical standards, previously found in the more expensive line of cars, were incorporated.

The OM 615 diesel engine had been altered but slightly, engine speed at 100 kilometers per hour was now 3,395 instead of 3,375, but maximum speed of the car remained the same despite an increase of 25 kilograms in weight. Acceleration was 1 second slower than before. Fuel consumption was 8.3 liters for 100 kilometers, up 0.2 from the previous model which gave 29 miles to the gallon of fuel oil.

All of the diesel engines now had the oil filter placed so that it could be changed from above, and a new type cylinder head gasket required no maintenance.

The older model was still in production to ease the great demand for the diesel cars, and 21,081 units were sold in 1976 when nearly 37,000 of the new W123 body style models were also manufactured. From December 1975 until 1979 a total of 135,470 units of the 200D were built.

In 1976 the W115 type 200D sold for DM 17,182.80, and the W123 model for DM 18,870. The next year the price was DM 19,536, in 1979 it was DM 21,347.20, and in 1980 the 200D sedan sold for DM 23,029.40.

Production of the 200D model [110] (from July 1965 until February 1968)

was in	1965	30,937 units
	1966	61,707 units
	1967	68,399 units
	1968	575 units
	total	161,618 units

Production of the 200D model [115 D20] (from October 1967/January 1968 until December 1976)

was in	1967	106 units
	1968	23,293 units
	1969	27,663 units
	1970	32,841 units
	1971	35,000 units
	1972	41,065 units
	1973	45,287 units
	1974	50,613 units
	1975	62,978 units
	1976	21,081 units
	total	339,927 units

Production of the 200D model [123] (from December 1975/January 1976)

was in	1975	5 units
	1976	36,894 units
	1977	56,378 units
	1978	49,359 units
	1979	52,834 units
	1980	56,435 units
	total	251,905 units

The instrument panel of the 1976 model

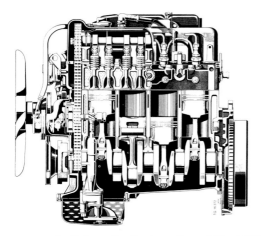 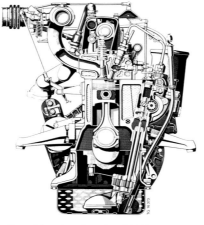 

Left: **Longitudinal section of the OM615 diesel engine for the 200D.**
Right: **Cross section of the OM615 engine.**

The OM615 engine installation

Technical Data

	200D/8 *(W110)*	200D *(W115)*	200D *(W123)*
Engine type	4 cyl diesel, overhead camshaft (OM 621 VIII)	4 cyl diesel, overhead camshaft (OM 615)	4 cyl diesel, overhead camshaft (OM 615)
Bore and stroke	87 x 83.6mm (3.43 x 3.29 in)	87 x 83.6mm (3.43 x 3.29 in)	87 x 83.6mm (3.43 x 3.29 in)
Displacement	1988 cc (121.27 cu in)	1988 cc (121.27 cu in)	1988 cc (121.27 cu in)
Power output	55 hp (DIN) @ 4200 rpm (60 hp SAE)	55 hp (DIN) @ 4200 rpm (61 hp SAE @ 4200 rpm)	55 hp (DIN) @ 4200 rpm; 1979: 60 hp (DIN) @ 4400 rpm
Compression ratio	21:1	21:1	21:1
Torque	11.5 mkg @ 2400 rpm (12 mkg SAE 87 ft/lbs)	11.5 mkg @ 2400 rpm (83.2 ft/lb)	11.5 mkg @ 2400 rpm (83.2 ft/lb)
Fuel injection	Bosch injection pump	Bosch four plunger pump	Bosch four plunger pump
Maximum engine speed	4320 rpm	5300 rpm	5300 rpm
Engine speed at 100 km/hr	3300 rpm	3375 rpm	3395 rpm automatic: 3470 rpm
Gear ratios	I. 4.09:1 automatic: I. 3.98:1 II. 2.25:1 II. 2.52:1 III. 1.42:1 III. 1.58:1 IV. 1.00:1 IV. 1.00:1	I. 3.90:1 II. 2.30:1 III. 1.41:1 IV. 1.00:1	I. 3.90:1 automatic: I. 3.98:1 II. 2.30:1 II. 2.39:1 III. 1.41:1 III. 1.46:1 IV. 1.00:1 IV. 1.00:1
Rear axle ratio	3.92	3.92 (for U.S. 4.08)	3.92
Chassis	unit frame and body	unit frame and body	unit frame and body
Suspension	independent front, single joint swing axle rear, with coil springs air suspension, optional	independent front and rear, with coil springs, diagonal-pivot swing axle, anti-sway bars	independent front and rear, with coil springs; diagonal swing axle, coil springs, anti-roll bar. Optional level control; standard in 1979
Brakes and area	disc front; drum, rear, servo assist, 253/230mm (9.96/9.06 in) two circuit hydraulic	disc, power assisted standard, 273/279mm (10.75/10.99 in)	dual circuit discs, power assisted, front brake pad wear indicator, 278/279mm (10.9/11.0 in)

74

The 200D sedan of 1976

	200D/8 *(W110)*	200D *(W115)*	200D *(W123)*
Wheelbase	2700mm (106.3 in)	2750mm (108.3 in)	2795mm (110.0 in)
Track, front/rear	1482/1485mm (58.3/58.5 in)	1440/1434mm (56.7/56.5 in)	1488/1466mm (58.6/56.9 in)
Length	4730mm (186.5 in)	4680mm (184.3 in)	4725mm (186.0 in)
Width	1795mm (70.7 in)	1770mm (69.7 in)	1786mm (70.3 in)
Height	1495mm (58.8 in)	1440mm (56.7 in)	1438mm (56.6 in)
Ground clearance	185mm (7.3 in)	175mm (6.9 in)	
Tires	7.00 x 13	6.95 x 14 or 175 x 14	175 SR 14
Turning circle	11.8–11.6 meters (39 ft)	11.7 meters (38.4 ft)	11.25 meters (36.9 ft); 1979: 11.29 meters (37 ft)
Steering type and ratio	recirculating ball, 22.7:1 (4.1 turns); servo assisted 17.3:1 (3.2 turns)	recirculating ball (4.6 turns); servo assisted (4.0 turns)	recirculating ball (4.0 turns); servo assisted
Weight	1325 kg (2915 lbs)	1350 kg (2970 lbs)	1375 kg (3025 lbs)
Maximum speed	130 km/hr (81 mph)	130 km/hr (81 mph)	130 km/hr (81 mph); automatic: 125 km/hr (78 mph) 1979: 135 km/hr (84 mph) automatic: 130 km/hr (81 mph)
Acceleration	29 sec 0–100 km/hr; automatic: 30 sec 0–100 km/hr	30 sec 0–100 km/hr	31 sec 0–100 km/hr; automatic: 33.2 sec; 1979: 27.4 sec; automatic: 29.4 sec
Fuel consumption	9 liters/100 km (26 mpg); automatic: 10 liter/100 km (23 mpg)	8.1 liters/100 km (29 mpg)	8.3 liters/100 km (28 mpg); 1979: at 120 km/hr 10.2 liters, automatic: 11.7 liters
Fuel tank capacity	65 liters (17.2 gallons)	65 liters (17.2 gallons)	65 liters (17.2 gallons)

The 220D sedan of 1973

Model 220D

The initial pre-production 220D model was actually built in July 1967, fully 3 months before the 200D. It was naturally of the New Generation— W115—body style which it shared with the 200 line and, of course, the 220 gasoline version.

All of these cars had the newly designed bodies, featuring a lower silhouette, lower center of gravity, and wider radiator design and were considered quite handsome indeed. They also had numerous detailed interior and outside features, and the larger displacement models were slightly more elegantly outfitted.

The OM 615 diesel engine for this model had been increased to become the 220D, but the previous 200D model was still available in Europe. In the United States, the 220D replaced the smaller 200D.

This 2,197 cubic centimeter (134.0 inches cubic) engine had a bore of 87 millimeters (3.43 inches) and a stroke of 92.4 millimeters (3.64 inches). Torque was 12.8 meters/kilogram, or 92.6 pounds/feet at 2,400 revolutions per minute. It was still basically the same four-cylinder single overhead camshaft engine with five main bearings. The pre-combustion chamber and cylinder head were redesigned for improved cooling and the new crankshaft had larger counter weights effecting less vibration. The aluminum pistons had four rings—three of them were plated with molybdenum for wear resistance and the fourth ring, the oil ring, was chrome plated. A steel insert was placed on the lower ring for faster break-in and reduced oil consumption. The engine developed 60 DIN, or 65 SAE, horsepower at 4,200 revolutions per minute. The compression ratio was 21 to 1.

A newly designed four-speed all-synchromeshed transmission was fitted. The rear axle ratio was 3.92:1, but in the United States the cars had the 4.08 ratio. The alternator was a Bosch 14V-35 ampere unit, and the battery was rated for 88 ampere/hours and 12 volts.

The front suspension consisted of unequal-length A-arms, coil springs and telescopic shock absorbers, anti-sway bar, self-lubricating. The rear suspension was of the new Daimler-Benz patented diagonal pivot swing axle, coil springs, telescopic shock absorbers and anti-sway

Above: Front view of the 220D sedan, 1973 (note the headlight wipers).
Below: The OM615 diesel engine installation.

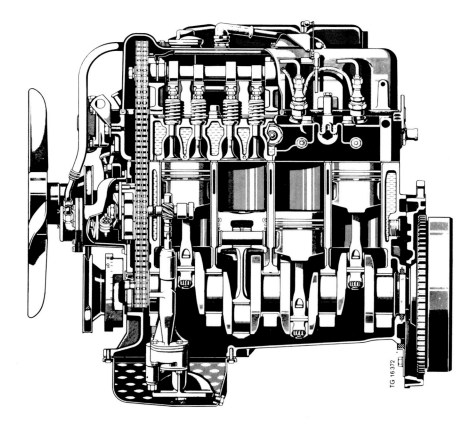

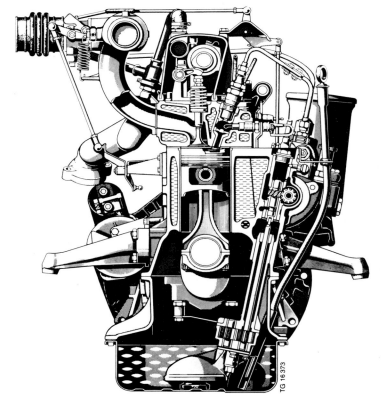

Upper left: Longitudinal section of the OM615 diesel engine of the 220D model. *Upper right:* Cross section of the OM615 diesel engine. *Left:* The OM615 diesel engine of the 220D.

bar. The tires were 6.95×14 (175×14) and were 4-ply rated, tubeless, mounted on 5½J rims.

The 220D had, of course, disc brakes on all four wheels. They were the caliper type with a separate drum-type parking brake. The brakes had a tandem master cylinder and servo power assistance as standard equipment. The diameter of the brakes was in front 10.75 inches and the rear 10.99 inches (273 and 279 millimeters, respectively).

The steering was of the recirculating ball type with rack and pinion and shock absorber. The ball joints were lubricated forever. The four-speed manual transmission was standard, either column or floor mounted. Automatic transmission was an optional extra, as were power brakes and power steering.

The 220D model passenger sedan weighed 2,997 pounds (1,363 kilograms). It had a wheelbase of 108.3 inches (2,750 millimeters) and was 184.3 inches (4,680 millimeters) long overall. Width was 69.7 inches (1,770 millimeters), height 56.7 inches (1,440 millimeters), and ground clearance 6.9 inches (175 millimeters). (The wheelbase was actually longer than that of the 190 model but the overall length shorter than that former model.) The fuel tank held 17.2 gallons (65 liters). Maximum and cruising speed were 135 kilometers (84 miles) per hour. With a fuel consumption of 27.75 miles to a gallon of diesel fuel, the cruising range was 477 miles. (The car used 8.5 liters per 100 kilometers.)

The price of the 220D four-door sedan in 1968 was in Germany DM 12,500, but in 1973 the price had risen to DM 15,485. In the United States the 220D sold in January 1968 for $4,494, but in 1973 (east coast) for $6,662.

From July 1967 until December 1976 production of this popular model was a total of 420,273 units. During the ten years when both models, the 200D and the 220D were sold, this larger model outsold the smaller one by 80,346 units or almost 20 percent.

Although the usual clattering when starting a cold diesel engine was somewhat diminished, it was still noticeable. And when idling one was certainly aware of the peculiar knock. Yet the tremendous economic operating savings made it an ever more popular and highly desirable automobile in this country, and sales were only limited by the scant availabaility of the model. In 1973 many more than the 5,000 diesel automobiles (of the 220D model) could have been sold in the

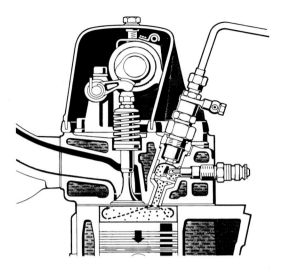

Above: Drawing of the pre-combustion chamber of the OM615. **Below:** Drawing of the fully independent diagonal pivot rear axle of the 220D.

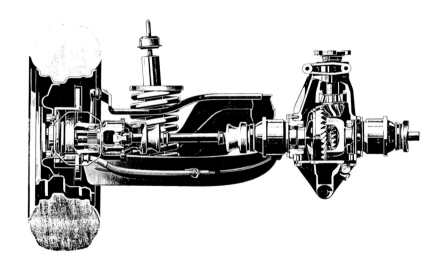

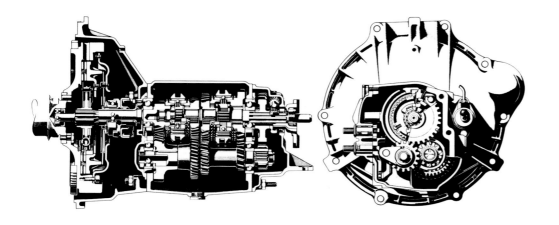

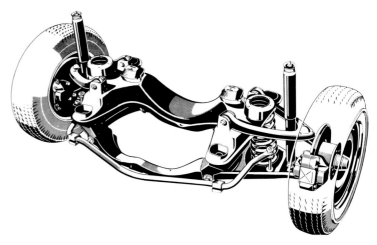

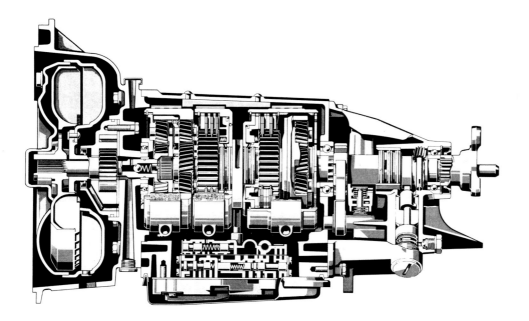

Drawing of the manual transmission and clutch (*above*) and drawing of the automatic transmission (*below*) for the New Generation W115 body style.

Drawing of the front axle and suspension (*above*) and drawing of the rear axle and suspension (*below*) of the W115 body.

United States were it not for the restriction caused by production of these vehicles by Daimler-Benz. (A total of 6,252 diesel-engined cars of all models were sold here.) Over a million diesel-engined passenger cars had been built by 1968 at the factory since 1949, proving the popularity of such vehicles. They had represented usually about 40 percent of the total production of automobiles over the years.

The diesel engine met the United States stringent emission control standards for hydrocarbons, carbon monoxide, and oxides of nitrogen for 1975. In fact, it was the only car engine in 1968, imported or domestic, to do that. A report by the Environmental Protection Agency in November 1973 stated that the 220D model showed 75 percent greater fuel economy than the average delivered by the 1973 gasoline-engined cars of the same weight class. The diesel engine, because of its more complete combustion process, produced lower air pollutants without the need for additional emission controls. (In fact, it produced one-half as much oxides of nitrogen, one-fifth as much hydrocarbon, and one-tenth as much carbon monoxide as a gasoline engine.)

A long wheelbase sedan, actually a limousine, became available in December 1968. It had seats for eight passengers and was similar to the 230 long limousine. The wheelbase was 3,400 millimeters (133.86 inches), and weight was 1,540 kilograms (3,388 pounds). The maximum speed was 130 kilometers (81 miles) per hour and fuel consumption was 11 liters per 100 kilometers (21 miles per gallon). With the optional automatic transmission, these figures were 125 kilometers per hour and 12 liters (18 miles per gallon), respectively.

Symbolic of the fantastic popularity of the diesel-engined automobiles, on May 9, 1968, the two millionth passenger automobile to come off the assembly lines at the Sindelfingen plant since 1946, when production of cars was again resumed after the war, was a 220D model. It was cream colored and bountifully decorated with fresh flowers for this historic event.

In 1971 the gasoline engine for the 220 sedan developed 100 horsepower while the diesel engine developed 57 horsepower. But three years later the gasoline engine, burdened by emission control devices with a lowered compression ratio (from 9:1 to 8:1) developed only 85 horsepower. The diesel engine, on the other hand, retained the same power output. Similar examples could be cited with other equal-sized power units. The ultimate adjustments and emission control limits were not yet reached, but the trend was unmistakenly clear. The diesel

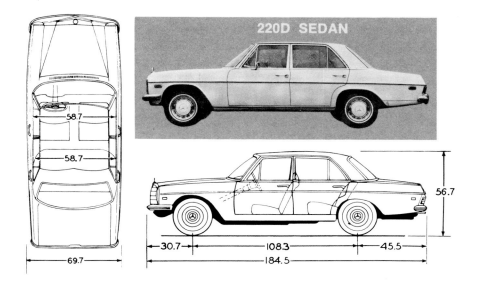

Dimensions of the 220D sedan of 1970

The instrument panel with console of the 220D

The 220D sedan of 1976

The injection part of the OM615 diesel engine

engine had a decided advantage over the gasoline unit in that it was not penalized as much in regards to emissions.

In 1976 the 220D also got the same new body—W123—as the smaller diesel-engined model. This so far best selling intermediate diesel—sales were over 420,000 units of the W115 model, with about 340,000 for the 200D and nearly 131,000 for the 240D—fell behind now, with the increased popularity of the newer five-cylinder diesel-engined 3-liter sedan.

The 2,197-cubic-centimeter engine developed five more horse-power than the 2-liter unit, and the actual weight of the two cars was within 5 kilograms of each other. Acceleration of the 220D was 28.1 seconds for the 0-100 kilometers per hour, about 3 seconds faster, and maximum speed was 5 kilometers faster than the 200D. Other differences were the fuel consumption, 9 against 8.3 liters for 100 kilometers of driving, and the power-to-weight ratio was 25 kilograms per horsepower for the 200D against 23 for the 220D.

These slight differences between the two models added to make the 220D a rather unpopular choice. And consequently the 220D model was discontinued in early 1979.

In 1976 the W115 type 220D sold for DM 17,848.80, and the newer W123 model for DM 19,558.20. A year later that price had risen to DM 20,346.30.

Production of the 220D model [115 D22] (from July 1967/January 1968 until December 1976)

was in	1967	364 units
	1968	50,630 units
	1969	59,628 units
	1970	63,314 units
	1971	64,297 units
	1972	73,729 units
	1973	54,321 units
	1974	27,510 units
	1975	21,226 units
	1976	5,254 units
	total	420,273 units

Production of the 220D model [123] (from December 1975/January 1976 until March 1979)

was in	1975	4 units
	1976	16,733 units
	1977	19,323 units
	1978	19,230 units
	1979	1,446 units
	total	56,736 units

Technical Data

	220D (W115)	220D (W123)
Engine type	4 cyl diesel, overhead camshaft (OM 615)	4 cyl diesel, overhead camshaft (OM 615)
Bore and stroke	87.0 x 92.4mm (3.43 x 3.64 in)	87.0 x 92.4mm (3.43 x 3.64 in)
Displacement	2197 cc (134 cu in)	2197 cc (134 cu in)
Power output	60 hp (DIN) (65 hp SAE) @ 4200 rpm	60 hp (DIN) @ 4200 rpm
Compression ratio	21:1	21:1
Torque	12.8 mkg @ 2400 rpm (92.6 ft/lb)	12.8 mkg @ 2400 rpm (92.6 ft/lb)
Fuel injection	Bosch four plunger pump	Bosch four plunger pump
Engine speed at 100 km/hr	3375 rpm	3395 rpm automatic: 3470 rpm
Gear ratios	I. 3.90:1 (15.37) II. 2.30:1 (9.01) III. 1.41:1 (5.52) IV. 1.00:1 (3.92)	I. 3.90:1 automatic: I. 3.98:1 II. 2.30:1 II. 2.39:1 III. 1.41:1 III. 1.46:1 IV. 1.00:1 IV. 1.00:1
Rear axle ratio	3.92 (for U.S. 4.08)	3.92
Chassis	unit frame and body	unit frame and body
Suspension	independent front and rear, with coil springs, diagonal-pivot swing axle, anti-sway bars	independent front and rear, with coil springs; diagonal swing axle, coil springs, anti-roll bar. Optional level control; standard in 1979
Brakes and area	disc, power assist standard, 273/279mm (10.75/10.99 in)	dual circuit discs, power assisted, front brake pad wear indicator, 278/279mm (10.9/11.0 in)
Wheelbase	2750mm (108.3 in)	2795mm (110.0 in)
Track, front/rear	1440/1434mm (56.7/56.5 in)	1488/1466mm (58.6/56.9 in)
Length	4680mm (184.3 in)	4725mm (186.0 in)
Width	1770mm (69.7 in)	1786mm (70.3 in)
Height	1440mm (56.7 in)	1438mm (56.6 in)
Ground clearance	175mm (6.9 in)	
Tires	6.95 x 14 or 175 x 14	175 SR 14
Turning circle	11.7 meters (38.4 ft)	11.25 meters (36.9 ft)
Steering type and ratio	recirculating ball (4.6 turns); servo assisted 22.7:1 (4.0 turns)	recirculating ball (4.0 turns); servo assisted
Weight	1363 kg (2997 lbs)	1380 kg (3036 lbs)
Maximum speed	135 km/hr (84 mph); automatic: 125 km/hr (82 mph)	135 km/hr (84 mph); automatic: 130 km/hr (81 mph)
Acceleration	28.1 sec 0–100 km/hr	28.1 sec 0–100 km/hr; automatic: 29.1 sec
Fuel consumption	8.5 liters/100 km (27.75 mpg)	9.0 liters/100 km (26 mpg)
Fuel tank capacity	65 liters (17.2 gallons)	65 liters (17.2 gallons)

The 240D sedan of 1974

Model 240D

The 240D model with the W115 body was first shown at the 1973 Frankfurt Auto Show. It shared its body style with the other intermediate line of cars, but especially so with the 230/4 gasoline model, the other new model also then introduced to the public.

The further refined and slightly enlarged four-cylinder overhead camshaft OM 616 diesel engine—the cylinder head had larger intake and outlet valves for improved breathing and consequent better cooling—had a bore of 90.9 millimeters (3.58 inches) and stroke of 92.4 millimeters (3.64 inches) for a total displacement of 2,376 cubic centimeters (146.7 cubic inches). It developed 65 DIN, or 62 SAE, horsepower at 4,000 revolutions per minute. Maximum engine speed allowable was 4,350 revolutions per minute. The torque was 14 meter/kilogram (97 pounds/feet) at 2,400 revolutions per minute. The compression ratio was 21 to 1. And all of the diesel engines had now a somewhat larger oil capacity than previously.

The crankshaft had five main bearings, coated with aluminum alloy. The fuel injection system was also the same as previously, the trusted Bosch four-plunger pump. The battery was an 88 ampere/hour type of 12 volts.

The cooling system held 21 pints. The thermostat was no longer located at the cooling water outlet, but instead at the inlet of the engine, resulting therefore in an increase in temperature during the warming-up period. This was especially beneficial in short-distance operation and added to the engine life. Next to the water cooler was an air-oil cooler.

The regular four-speed manual fully synchronized transmission with floor shift, making especially for a most economical operation, was standard but a newly designed four-speed automatic torque converter transmission was available as an option. Ratios were 3.90 in first, 2.30 in second, 1.41 in third, and 1.00 in fourth gear. It was geared to the torque characteristics and offered maximum driving comfort since gear changes were hardly noticeable under normal driving conditions. The rear axle ratio was 3.69:1.

Basically this 240D car was the same as the previous models, the 200D and 220D lines of 1967, but the radiator grille was slightly lower and 10 centimeters wider. As an added safety measure, the rear lights

The 240D sedan of 1975 for the U.S.

were so ridged that they remained visible longer under splash conditions, the outside mirror was adjustable from the inside, moldings on the windshield pillars diverted rain water away from the side windows for improved visibility under such conditions, and a special channel over the rear window was so designed that it kept rain water from obscuring rear vision.

The chassis was of the unitized construction type. The body was welded to the frame-floor unit. Suspension was of the usual kind. The independent front suspension consisted of double wishbones and anti-dive control. The wheel suspension was by coil springs with stabilizer bar and single tube gas-pressurized shock absorbers. The independent

Refinements of the New Generation body style:
Left: Windshield pillars divert rain water. *Lower
left:* Outside mirror adjustable from the inside.
Below: Rear lights ridged for better visibility
under splash conditions.

rear suspension had the proven Daimler-Benz diagonal swing axle and anti-lift control. Wheel suspension was the same as the front. The tires were 6.95×14 (175×14) radial whitewall tubeless, mounted on 5.5-inch rims.

The steering system was of the recirculating ball type gear segment and had the Mercedes-Benz power steering with steering shock absorber. The four-wheel power-assisted disc brakes were of the two-circuit hydraulic type, with 273/279 millimeter (10.8/11.0 inch) front and rear braking areas.

The wheelbase of the car was 108.3 inches (2,750 millimeters) with a track in front of 57.0 inches (1,448 millimeters) and rear of 56.7 inches (1,440 millimeters). The overall length was 195.5 inches in the United States version (184.3 inches, or 4,680 millimeters in the others), and ground clearance was 6.8 inches (175 millimeters). The width of the sedan was 69.7 inches (1,770 millimeters) and turning circle was 11 meters (36 feet).

The 240D weighed 3,205 pounds (1,457 kilograms) in the U.S. version which was introduced to the American market in November 1973. Elsewhere the weight was 1,390 kilograms (3,058 pounds). Outwardly it was quite indistinguishable from the other smaller Mercedes-Benz models, such as the 230 and 280 line of 1974.

Performance was substantially improved over the older models, despite the more direct axle reduction ratio. Acceleration from a standstill to 100 kilometers per hour (62 miles) was 24.6 seconds against the 28.1 figure of the 220D, or even the 30 seconds for the 200D model. (Of course, the horsepower differential was 65, 60, and 55.) The maximum speed of the 240D was 138 kilometers (85.7 miles) as to the 135 kilometers (84 miles) of the 220D and 130 kilometers (81 miles) per hour for the 200D.

The fuel tank held 17.2 gallons (65 liters) with a reserve of 2.4 gallons, sufficient fuel to give the car a driving range well over 500 miles (800 kilometers). The Environmental Protection Agency rated the 240D at 31 miles per gallon for highway driving and 24 miles per gallon for city driving.

The price of the 240D sedan was in 1973, for the standard transmission type, DM 15,985, but in 1975 it was DM 18,425. In the United States the car sold for $8,140 (east coast) and the automatic transmission type for $8,715. The 1975 prices were $9,172 and $9,811, respectively. (In 1976 the 240D sold for $10,621, at the east coast). A total of

The OM616 diesel engine of the 240D, 1973

131,391 units of the 240D were built from February 1973 until December 1976.

In a sales brochure of that time, the greater elasticity of the engine of the 240D model was prominently stressed and compared to the other available diesel models. Better acceleration was one of the benefits of this change in engine size. It suggested that surely one of the three different models could satisfy any prospective buyer of that type of automobile. Using 30 percent less fuel than the comparable gasoline engine, there was also a saving in lower insurance premiums. As to the reliability, a survey showed that 78 percent of all diesel models built since 1946 were still in use in Germany, a truly impressive record.

And, in August 1973, the larger 240D engine was installed in the long-wheelbase limousine to improve the performances of that special vehicle. It was just a natural, progressive step. All of the specifications of the earlier model applied to this one, except that the maximum speed

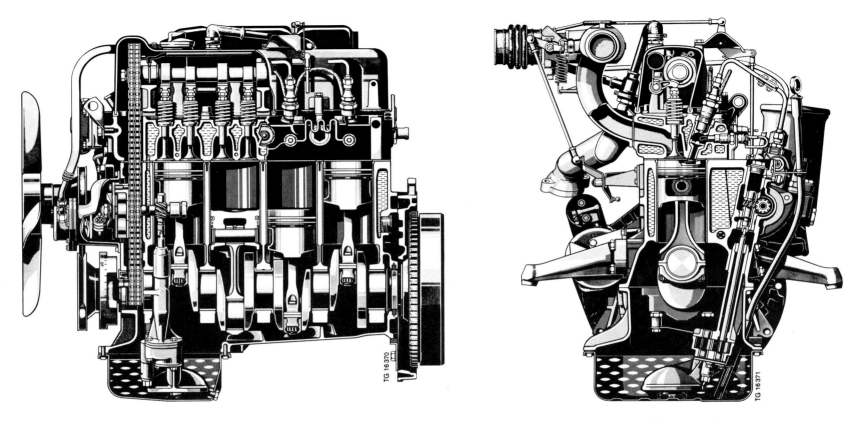

Left: **Longitudinal section of the OM616 diesel engine of the 240D.** *Right:* **Cross section of the OM616 engine.**

was now 135 kilometers (84 miles) per hour, and with the automatic transmission 130 kilometers (81 miles) per hour. Fuel consumption was 11.5 liters (20.4 miles per gallon), and 12.5 liters (18.75 miles per gallon), respectively, for 100 kilometers. The overall weight had also increased by 15 kilograms, to 1,555 kilograms (3,421 pounds) for the vehicle.

The 240D was the third of the diesel models to get the new W123 body in 1976. Here too, the older model style was still being manufactured to ease the tremendous demand of these economical diesel sedans.

The wheelbase—of all of the 123 model styles—was 45 millime-ters (1.8 inches) longer than the previous ones and the front axle track 40 millimeters (1.6 inches) wider to give improved comfort and better roadholding. The bumpers had rubber guards and side strips with rubber inlets protected the body from negligent and careless opening of doors of too closely parked cars. Windshield wipers were parallel running instead of the formerly butterfly style and were black to prevent reflections. Seat belts had been repositioned for improved comfort and safety. The heating and ventilating system was simplified and made more efficient, and the easy-to-read panel with round instruments had a heavily inclined glass plate which eliminated glare and was easier to

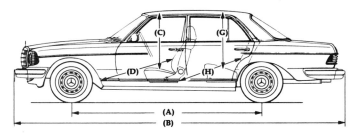

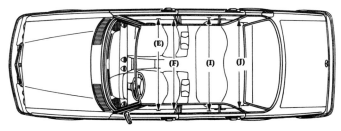

Interior Dimensions
240 D

Wheelbase (in./mm.)	(A)	110.0/2795
Overall Length (in./mm.)	(B)	190.9/4848
Head Room Front (in./mm.)	(C)	38.3/973
Leg Room Front (in./mm.)	(D)	41.9/1064
Hip Room Front (in./mm.)	(E)	58.1/1476
Shoulder Room Front (in./mm.)	(F)	56.0/1422
Head Room Rear (in./mm.)	(G)	37.3/948
Leg Room Rear (in./mm.)	(H)	33.5/850
Hip Room Rear (in./mm.)	(I)	58.3/1480
Shoulder Room Rear (in./mm.)	(J)	55.7/1416

Dimensions of the 240D sedan of 1981

Below: The 240D sedan of 1976. *Above:* The 240D sedan of 1979 for the U.S.

keep clean. And a simpler key-operated starter was available by 1977 instead of the former pull knob system. The car weighed somewhat more now, 1,477 kilograms (3,250 pounds).

Acceleration figures given for the 0 to 100 kilometers per hour were 24.6 seconds, and with automatic transmission 27.4 seconds. This was improved slightly, when the following year, 1980, the figures were 22.0 seconds (automatic: 24.7 seconds). For that model year, however, the power output had been raised, in the cars for the United States, to 67 SAE horsepower, but the sedan now weighed 1,415 kilograms (3,120 pounds).

For 1979 the Environmental Protection Agency rated the 240D at 30 miles per gallon for city and 34 miles per gallon for highway driving, or an average fuel consumption figure of 30 miles per gallon. With the automatic transmission, the figures were 27 for the city driving cycle. For 1980 Environmental Protection Agency figures were 28 for city and 34 for highway driving, or a combined rating of 30 miles per gallon. With the

automatic transmission, the figures were 26 and 29, or a 27 miles per gallon rating combination.

For the 1981 model year, these ratings were 29 for city and 33 for highway driving, and with the automatic transmission 27 and 31 miles per gallon, respectively.

The longer wheelbase (LW) car (3,425 millimeters, or 134.8 inches) was also available in 1979, in the newer styled body type. The basic specifications were those for the regular 240D, except for the track (1,477/1,430 millimeters, or 58.1/56.3 inches), the overall length (5,355 millimeters, or 210.8 inches), and height (1,480 millimeters, or 58.3 inches), and the turning circle of 13.35 meters (43.8 feet). The rear suspension of this limousine had a leveling control device as standard equipment.

Production of the 240D four-door sedan, from December 1975 until 1979 was a total of 167,130 units.

In 1976 the 240D in the W115 body style sold for DM 18,426. and the newer W123 model was DM 20,146.50. The following year the 240D sold for DM 21,056.70, in 1979 for DM 22,825.60, and in 1980 for DM 24,600.10. The long-wheelbase 240D sold in 1976 for DM 26,073.90, in 1977 for DM 33,100.20, in 1979 for DM 35,940.80, and in 1980 for DM 38,612.10.

In the United States the 240D, with manual transmission, sold in 1979 for $15,068 (east coast), in 1980 for $17,533, and in 1981 for $19,312. With the automatic transmission the price, in 1981, was $20,558 (east coast).

Comparison with the regular wheelbase 240D sedan

Production of the 240D model [115 D24] (from February/August 1973 until December 1976)

was in	1973	16,512 units
	1974	60,928 units
	1975	38,019 units
	1976	15,860 units
	total	131,319 units

Production of the 240D model [123] (from December 1975/January 1976)

was in	1975	7 units
	1976	21,247 units
	1977	40,382 units
	1978	42,816 units
	1979	62,678 units
	1980	69,908 units
	total	237,038 units

Above: The instrument panel of the 240D of 1979. *Below:* The 240D sedan of 1981 for the U.S. *Left:* The new four-speed transmission of 1980.

The long-wheelbase sedan for 7 to 8 passengers

Technical Data

	240D (W115)	240D (W123)	240D (LW) (W123)
Engine type	4 cyl diesel, overhead camshaft (OM 616)	4 cyl diesel, overhead camshaft (OM 616)	*In 1979 the 240D model became also available with a longer wheelbase as an eight-passenger limousine.*
Bore and stroke	91 x 92.4mm (3.58 x 3.64 in)	91 x 92.4mm (3.58 x 3.64 in) 1979: 90.9 x 92.4mm	*The basic specifications were as those of the regular model, but with the following exceptions:*
Displacement	2376 cc (146.7 cu in)	2402 cc (146.7 cu in) 1979: 2399 cc (146.4 cu in)	
Power output	65 hp (DIN) @ 4200 rpm (62 hp SAE @ 4000 rpm)	65 hp (DIN) @ 4200 rpm; 1977: 64 hp 1979: 72 hp (DIN) @ 4400 rpm U.S. 1977: 62 hp SAE @ 4000 rpm U.S. 1980: 67 hp (SAE) @ 4000 rpm	
Compression ratio	21:1	21:1	
Torque	14 mkg @ 2400 rpm (13.4 mkg 97 ft/lb @ 2400 rpm)	14 mkg @ 2400 rpm (101.3 ft/lb) U.S. 1977: 13.4 mkg @ 2400 rpm (97 ft/lb)	
Fuel injection	Bosch four plunger pump	Bosch four plunger pump	
Maximum engine speed		5400 rpm; 1979: 5300 rpm; U.S. 1977: 4350 rpm U.S. 1980: 4000 rpm	
Engine speed at 100 km/hr	3180 rpm	3195 rpm; automatic: 3275 rpm	

Technical Data

	240D (W115)	240D (W123)	240D (LW) (W123)
Gear ratios	I. 3.90:1 II. 2.30:1 III. 1.41:1 IV. 1.00:1	I. 3.90:1 automatic: I. 3.98:1 II. 2.30:1 II. 2.39:1 III. 1.41:1 III. 1.46:1 IV. 1.00:1 IV. 1.00:1	
Rear axle ratio	3.69	3.69	
Chassis	unit frame and body	unit frame and body	
Suspension	independent front and rear, double wishbones, diagonal-pivot swing axle, anti-sway bars	independent front and rear, with coil springs; diagonal swing axle, coil springs, anti-roll bar. Optional level control; standard in 1979	
Brakes and area	disc, hydraulic dual circuit, 273/279mm (10.8/11.0 in)	dual circuit discs, power assisted, front brake pad wear indicator, 278/279 mm (10.9/11.0 in)	
Wheelbase	2750mm (108.3 in)	2795mm (110.0 in)	3425mm (134.8 in)
Track, front/rear	1448/1440mm (57.0/56.7 in)	1488/1466mm (58.6/56.9 in)	1477/1430mm (58.1/56.3 in)
Length	4680mm (184.3 in); U.S.: 195.5 in	4725mm (186.0 in) U.S. 1977: 4848mm (190.9 in)	5355mm (210.8 in)
Width	1770mm (69.7 in)	1786mm (70.3 in)	
Height	1440mm (56.7 in)	1438mm (56.6 in)	1480mm (58.3 in)
Ground clearance	175mm (6.9 in)		
Rear suspension			level control standard
Tires	175 SR 14	175 SR 14	
Turning circle	11 meters (36.1 ft)	11.25 meters (36.9 ft) 1979: 11.29 meters (37 ft) U.S. 1977: 11.29 meters (37 ft)	13.35 meters (43.8 ft)
Steering type and ratio	recirculating ball (3.0 turns), servo assisted	recirculating ball (4.0 turns); servo assisted U.S. 1977: 2.7 turns; U.S. 1980: 3.2 turns	
Weight	1390 kg (3058 lbs); U.S.: 1457 kg (3205 lbs)	1385 kg (3047 lbs) U.S. 1977: 1455 kg (3210 lbs) U.S. 1980: 1415 kg (3120 lbs)	1565 kg (3443 lbs)
Maximum speed	138 km/hr (85.7 mph) automatic: 133 km/hr (82.6 mph)	138 km/hr (86 mph) automatic: 133 km/hr (83 mph) 1979: 143 km/hr (89 mph) automatic: 138 km/hr (86 mph)	
Acceleration	24.6 sec 0–100 km/hr	24.6 sec 0–100 km/hr; automatic: 27.4 sec 1979: 22.0 sec; automatic: 24.7 sec	0–100 km/hr: 24.6 sec automatic: 27.2 sec
Fuel consumption	9.5 liters/100 km (24.75 mpg)	9.5 liters/100 km (24.75 mpg); 1979: at 120 km/hr: 10.9 liters; automatic: 11.4 liters	at 120 km/hr: 11.1 liters automatic: 12.2 liters
Fuel tank capacity	65 liters (17.2 gallons) 1976: 80 liters (20.6 gallons)	65 liters (17.2 gallons) U.S. 1977: 80 liters (21.1 gallons) U.S. 1980: 65 liters (17.2 gallons)	

The 300D sedan for the United States, 1974

Model 300D

The presentation of the 240D 3.0 model in July 1974 created tremendous interest. (Designated as the 300D, the car was introduced in December 1974 in the United States.) The five-in-line cylinder configuration seemed truly a revolutionary engineering feat and attracted immense attention and wide comment.

It was a bold decision to construct such an unorthodox engine for a passenger car, but chief engineer Hans Scherenberg was able to solve the intricate problem of achieving the critical balance of that peculiar construction. More power was needed for a diesel-engined car and while increasing the existing smaller 200D engine to a six-cylinder unit would have solved that problem quite simply, it was impossible to fit such an enlarged engine into the chassis of the current passenger car models. The total engine weight was also a crucial factor to be considered and adding one more cylinder to the 240D power plant was therefore a preferred and rather logical solution. The displacement of 600 cubic centimeters per cylinder was considered ideal. Daimler-Benz had been using a five-cylinder diesel engine in some of their truck models for some years.

In passenger cars, a five-cylinder engine had been first used in 1906 by Adams-Farwell. That was a radial engine rotating around a fixed crankshaft. And a Swiss manufacturer had built a vehicle with an air-cooled engine during the 1920s. But the 300D was the first passenger car to use an in-line five-cylinder diesel engine.

Basically the five-cylinder OM 617 diesel engine utilized all of the parts of the chain-driven single overhead camshaft four-cylinder unit. (Firing order was 1, 2, 4, 5, 3 of the cylinders.) The bore of 90.9 millimeters (3.58 inches) and stroke of 92.5 millimeters (3.64 inches) displaced 3,006 cubic centimeters (183.4 cubic inches) and developed 80 DIN, or 77 SAE, horsepower at 4,000 revolutions per minute. The compression ratio was 21 to 1. Torque was 16 meters/kilogram (115.7 pounds/feet) at 2,400 revolutions per minute. The engine weighed 515 pounds, just 68 pounds more than the four-cylinder unit.

The 300D had only the automatic transmission and no manual system was made available in this novel automobile. The rear axle ratio was 3.46:1, giving the car a maximum speed of 148 kilometers (92 miles) per hour. (The United States version produced only 143 kilometers, or 89 miles, per hour.) The gear ratios were 3.98 in first, 2.39 in second, 1.46 in third, and 1.00 in fourth.

Performance figures showed better results than for the four-cylinder car. Acceleration from 0 to 100 kilometers (62 miles) per hour was 19.9 seconds, nearly five seconds faster than the 24.6 seconds of the 240D. The maximum speed of 148 kilometers per hour was 10 kilometers faster than that of the 240D. Engine performance was smooth and there were no drivability problems as with gasoline-engined cars, because no emission control devices were required on the diesel engine to hamper the designed smoothness of operation. To eliminate the rich mixture in altitude driving, a compensation knob was installed to vary the amount of fuel supplied for the injectors at up to 4,000 feet normal, from 4,000 to 8,000 feet, and from 8,000 to 12,000 feet.

Hans Scherenberg
Chief Engineer
1963-1977

Above: The 240D 3.0 sedan of 1974. *Upper left:* The rear view of the 240 3.0, 1974. *Left:* Schematic Drawing of the 300D sedan.

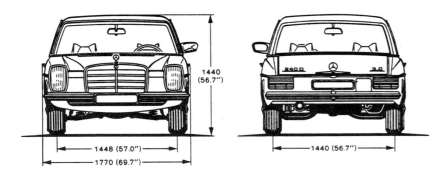

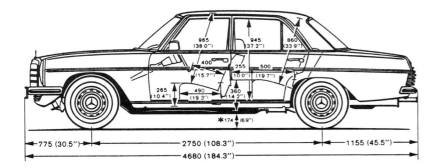

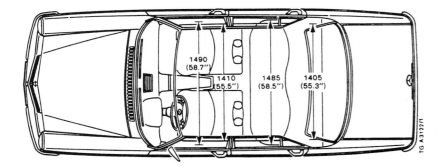

Illustrations showing the dimensions of the 300D sedan

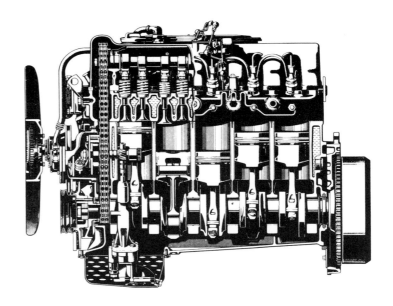

Above: Longitudinal section of the OM617 diesel engine. *Below:* The five piston arrangement for the same engine.

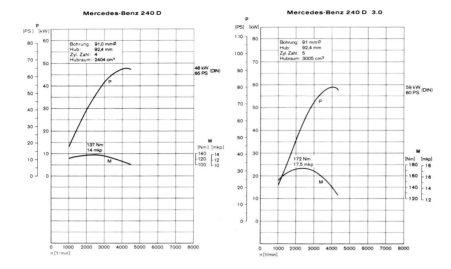

**Charts showing the power and torque curves of the
240D and the 240D 3.0/300D.**

Fuel consumption was 10.8 liters per 100 kilometers (21.5 miles per gallon). But the Environmental Protection Agency rated the fuel consumption for the 300D at 31 miles per gallon for highway driving, the same as for the 240D, and 24 miles per gallon for the city cycle. This impressive fuel economy was for the five-passenger sedan with automatic transmission and, of course, the several power-consuming accessories.

The diesel engine met the Federal anti-pollution requirements without emission controls. With the 17.2-gallon (65 liters) fuel tank, the driving range of the 300D would be in excess of 500 miles, a welcome fact to those who may have found it difficult to buy diesel fuel in their immediate localities and had to go beyond the city limits to fill their tanks. In 1976 a larger fuel tank, holding 80 liters (20.6 gallons) was provided.

The Bosch fuel injection pump was entirely redesigned. A centrifugal governor operated the metering rack and regulated the power output. The starting of the cold engine was decidedly easier than on previous diesel models, taking but a short time for the glow plug to

heat up. Cylinder crank head and housing, head gasket, and the six main bearing crankshaft and oil pan were also new.

All other technical specifications were shared with the 240D model. The weight of that car had increased from the newer 1975 model to 3,205 pounds and that of the 300D was 1.430 kilograms (3,146 pounds). (The United States version weighed 3,450 pounds.) Both diesel-engined cars shared with the 230 and 280 gasoline-engined models the luxury features of these smaller-sized W115 passenger car models.

However, in the United States the two diesel models differed in their standard equipment. Several items which were available on an optional basis in the 240D, were standard equipment in the larger-engined car. These items were the air conditioning unit, automatic transmission (manual was not offered at all), fog lights, power windows, and a radio.

The 240D 3.0 model sold in 1974 for DM 18,815 and in 1975 for DM 19,915. And in the United States the price for the 300D four door sedan was quoted as $11,782 at the east coast port of entry. In 1976 the car sold for $13,582 at east and Gulf coast ports, and by the end of 1977 the price was $16,107. From May 1974 until November 1976 a total of 53,690 units were produced.

Over the years, sales of diesel-engined Mercedes-Benz passenger cars in the United States had shown a steady increase. When first introduced here, they amounted to 15 percent of car sales, but were up to 26.5 percent in 1974. A total of 18,000 diesel-engined automobiles were expected to be sold by Mercedes-Benz of North America, the distributors, in 1975, the quantity being limited because of production. (Actually 18,578 units were sold, or 41 percent of total sales. In 1976 it was 20,044 units, or 46.4 percent.) The factory had, ever since after the war, built consistently about 40 percent of the entire passenger car production in diesel-engined models. (In 1976 it was 42.6 percent.) In September 1971 a million diesels had been built in Untertürkheim and Sindelfingen since 1949—a period of 22 years—but by July of 1975 a total of one-and-a-half million such cars had come off the assembly lines. Thus, in four years, production was half as much as in the 22 previous years.

It was estimated that over 65,000 Mercedes-Benz diesel passenger cars were in use in the United States then and that this new model would allow some of their owners to change to a more powerful and more luxurious one. It was also hoped that the 300D would appeal to many prospective gasoline model buyers. The fuel economy, durability, and especially the simplified maintenance of the diesel with no spark plugs to change and distributor to worry about, no ignition system to service, no tune-up, and no problems with vapor lock or hot starting problems, were added inducements to future car buyers to select a diesel-engined automobile.

The 300D got the W123 body style in 1976 which it shared with the other diesel models as well as the gasoline intermediate sedans. Although first introduced as the 240D 3.0 model, it was soon designated as 300D in Germany. As either one, however, this relative newcomer enjoyed great popularity. In mid-1977, the 100,000th five-cylinder diesel passenger car engine was built.

The new body had, as the others, the synchronized four-speed transmission with floor shift, or as an optional extra, the automatic four-speed with torque converter. (In the United States, the automatic transmission only was offered.) It had an improved, more rigid clutch bell housing and transmission case which reduced the bending vibration and made for smoother operation. The front had individual wheel suspension by means of double control arms, two coil springs, with additional rubber springs, hydraulic telescope shock absorbers and anti-roll bar. The rear had a diagonal pivot swing axle, two coiled springs with additional rubber springs, hydraulic shock absorbers and anti-roll bar. Level control was an optional extra.

The Environmental Protection Agency in 1979 rated the 300D at 23 miles per gallon for city driving and 28 for highway, or an average fuel consumption of 25 miles per gallon. The same figures applied to 1980. However, for California the rating for the stricter emission control cars was actually slightly better, 24 and 28, for a combined 26 miles per gallon average. But for 1981 the ratings were 24 and 28, respectively, for all states.

The 300D LW model was, as usual, available with the newer body style. Specifications were those of the regular model, but this 3,425 millimeter wheelbase six and eight passenger limousine weighed 1,615 kilograms (3,553 pounds) and fuel consumption was 12.4 liters for 100 kilometers.

In 1976 the W123 bodied 300D sedan sold for DM 22,311, in 1977 for DM 23,321.10, in 1979 for DM 24,897.60, and in 1980 the price was DM 27,176.50. The 300D long-wheelbase limousine sold in 1977 for

The 300D sedan of 1976

DM 34,698.60, in 1979 for DM 37,307.20, and in 1980 for DM 40,431.40.

In the United States the 300D sold in February 1979 for $20,911 (with automatic transmission), east coast. In 1981 the 300D sedan sold for $25,640 (east coast). From December 1975 until 1979 a total of 179,814 units of the 300D sedan were manufactured.

Production of the 240D 3.0 four-door sedan [115 D30] (from May 1974 until November 1976.)

	was in	1974	7,650 units
		1975	34,420 units
		1976	11,620 units
		total	53,690 units

Production of the 300D model [123] (from December 1975/January 1976)

	was in	1975	9 units
		1976	28,996 units
		1977	48,605 units
		1978	49,908 units
		1979	52,296 units
		1980	50,197 units
		total	230,011 units

Rear view of the 300D of 1976

Technical Data

	240D 3.0 / (300D) (W115)	300D (W123)	300D (LW) (W123)
Engine type	5 cyl diesel, overhead camshaft (OM 617)	5 cyl diesel, overhead camshaft (OM 617)	*In 1979 the 300D model became also available with a longer wheelbase as an eight-passenger limousine.*
Bore and stroke	91 x 92.4mm (3.58 x 3.64 in)	91 x 92.4mm (3.58 x 3.64 in) 1979: 90.9 x 92.4mm	*The basic specifications were as those of the regular model, but with the following exceptions:*
Displacement	2971 cc (183.4 cu in)	3055 cc (183.4 cu in) U.S. 1979: 2998 cc (183.0 cu in)	
Power output	80 hp (DIN) @ 4000 rpm (77 hp SAE @ 4000 rpm)	80 hp (DIN) @ 4000 rpm 1979: 88 hp (DIN) @ 4400 rpm U.S. 1977: 77 hp (SAE) @ 4000 rpm U.S. 1980: 83 hp (SAE) @ 4200 rpm	
Compression ratio	21:1	21:1	
Torque	17.5 mkg @ 2400 rpm 16 mkg @ 2400 rpm (115.7 ft/lb)	17.5 mkg @ 2400 rpm (126.6 ft/lb) U.S. 1977: 15.9 mkg @ 2400 rpm (115 ft/lb) U.S. 1980: 16.7 mkg @ 2400 rpm (120 ft/lb)	
Fuel injection	Bosch injector pump	Bosch five plunger pump	
Maximum engine speed		5100 rpm; 1979: 5300 rpm U.S. 1977: 4350 rpm; U.S. 1980: 4200 rpm	
Engine speed at 100 km/hr	2980 rpm		
Gear ratios	I. 3.98:1 (13.77) II. 2.39:1 (8.27) III. 1.46:1 (5.05) IV. 1.00:1 (3.46)	I. 3.90:1 automatic I. 3.98:1 II. 2.30:1 II. 2.39:1 III. 1.41:1 III. 1.46:1 IV. 1.00:1 IV. 1.00:1	
Rear axle ratio	3.46	3.46	
Chassis	unit frame and body	unit frame and body	
Suspension	independent front and rear, double wishbones, diagonal pivot swing axle	independent front and rear, with coil springs; diagonal swing axle, coil springs, anti-roll bar. Optional level control; standard in 1979	
Brakes and area	disc, front vented; rear solid, 273/279mm (10.8/11.0 in)	dual circuit discs, power assisted, front brake pad wear indicator (278/279mm (10.9/11.0 in)	

100

The 300D sedan of 1979, U.S. version

	240D 3.0 / (300D) *(W115)*	300D *(W123)*	300D (LW) *(W123)*
Wheelbase	2750mm (108.3 in)	2795mm (110.0 in)	3425mm (134.8 in)
Track, front/rear	1448/1440mm (57.0/56.7 in)	1488/1466mm (58.6/56.9 in)	1477/1430mm (58.1/56.3 in)
Length	4680mm (184.3 in); U.S.: 195.5 in	4725mm (186.0 in) U.S. 1977: 4848mm (190.9 in)	5355mm (210.8 in)
Width	1770mm (69.7 in)	1786mm (70.3 in)	
Height	1440mm (56.7 in)	1438mm (56.6 in)	1480mm (58.3 in)
Ground clearance	175mm (6.9 in)		
Rear suspension			level control standard
Tires	175 SR 14	175 SR 14	
Turning circle	11 meters (36.1 ft)	11.25 meters (36.9 ft) 1979: 11.29 meters (37 ft) U.S. 1977: 11.29 meters (37 ft)	13.35 meters (43.8 ft)
Steering type and ratio	recirculating ball (3.0 turns), servo assisted	recirculating ball (4.0 turns), servo assisted U.S. 1977: 2.7 turns; U.S. 1980: 3.2 turns	
Weight	1430 kg (3146 lbs); U.S.: 3450 lbs	1445 kg (3179 lbs) U.S. 1977: 1595 kg (3515 lbs) U.S. 1978: 1600 kg (3530 lbs) U.S. 1980: 1555 kg (3430 lbs)	1615 kg (3553 lbs)
Maximum speed	148 km/hr (92 mph); U.S.: 143 km/hr (89 mph)	148 km/hr (92 mph) automatic: 143 km/hr (89 mph) 1979: 155 km/hr automatic: 150 km/hr (93 mph)	
Acceleration	20.6 sec 0–100 km/hr	19.9 sec 0–100 km/hr automatic: 20.8 sec; 1979: 17.8 sec automatic: 19.2 sec	19.4 sec 0–100 km/hr automatic: 20.8 sec
Fuel consumption	10.8 liters/100 km (21.5 mph)	10.8 liters/100 km (21.5 mpg) 1979: at 120 km/hr 11.5 liters automatic: 12.4 liters	at 120 km/hr: 12.4 liters automatic: 12.0 liters
Fuel tank capacity	65 liters (17.2 gallons) 1976: 80 liters (20.6 gallons)	65 liters (17.2 gallons) U.S. 1977: 80 liters (21.1 gallons)	

101

The C111 record car in 1976 trim

Records for Turbocharged Diesels

To test the reliability of a turbo-charged engine and to determine the true limit of such a modification as well as observe its operational behavior during actual driving in a road car, rather than on a test stand in the laboratory, Daimler-Benz decided to run a slightly modified five-cylinder diesel engine on a race track.

Earlier, in October and November 1975, Fritz Busch had established several short distance speed records on a test track at Ehra-Lessien in the Luneburg Heath. The factory prepared turbo-charged five-cylinder 2,999 cubic centimeter diesel engine, developing 187 DIN horsepower at 4,500 revolutions per minute and with a torque of 36 meters/kilogram at 3,500 revolutions per minute, was installed in a highly streamlined wedge-shaped racing car. Busch drove the flying mile at 249.188 kilometers (about 154.8 miles) per hour. For the ¼ mile he drove 103.65 kilometers (64.41 miles) per hour, the ½ kilometer at 112.247 kilometers (69.74 miles) per hour, and the 1 kilometer distance at 136.116 kilometers (84.57 miles) per hour. His maximum speed was actually 253.705 kilometers (157.65 miles) per hour.

But the speed record effort made on June 12 to 14, 1976, by the factory, under the leadership of chief engineer Hans Scherenberg, was a much more ambitious undertaking.

The Daimler-Benz experimental C111 car (which had, since its introduction at the Frankfurt Auto Show in 1969, already covered well over 20,000 miles with the four-rotor Wankel engine) was modified with aerodynamic headlight fairings and solid wheel covers so that the air resistance coefficients were below 0.3. The tires fitted were 215/70X15. The 12.64-kilometer (7.85-mile) track selected was the SASN (Societa Autopiste Sperimentale di Nardo) near Nardo, southern Italy, where at various times other tests had also been made by the engineers on their prototypes and experimental developments.

The vehicle was driven by the engineers involved in that endurance and record breaking project, Joachim Kaden, Hans Liebold, Guido Moch, and Erich Waxenberger. Each man drove for two and a half hours at a time when the 37 gallon (140 liter) fuel tanks had to be

Above: The 190 DIN horsepower diesel engine turbocharged.
Below: The instrument panels for the driver of the C111.

103

	Federal + Californien 1977	300 D Serie USA 1977	Rekord-Motor OM 617 D 30 A/300 D Serie USA	
HC	1,5	0,29	0,2	
CO	15,0/9,0	1,00	1,4	
NOx	2,0	1,70	2,0	
	gpm	gpm	mpg	l/100 km

Comparison chart of emissions and fuel consumption

Frenzied, but well organized activity, of the crew at a refueling stop

refilled. That change and minor maintenance took between 20 and 30 seconds. In about 64 hours, sixteen international class records and three world speed records for land vehicles, class 8, were established, all considerably higher (by around 60 kilometers per hour) than previous ones.

The OM 617 engine was actually reduced slightly to a capacity of less than 3,000 cubic centimeters—to qualify for the class records—by minor alteration of the cylinder bore diameter. The compression was lowered, changes in camshaft timing were made, and a special Bosch injection pump was installed. Especially made pistons were pin-point cooled by an oil spray system. Several parts were made of a different material or were especially treated because of the expected increased stress on the units. However, remarkably, the crankshaft and main bearings were left identical with those of the regular production diesel engine.

The gas exhaust turbocharger T-04B, made by Garrett AiResearch, reached a maximum of 135,000 revolutions per minute and compressed the intake air to a boost pressure of about 2 kilograms per square centimeter. The air temperature of about 220° Celsius was reduced to about 100° Celsius (212 Fahrenheit). The unit was tuned to insure that the highest boost pressure was reached at an engine speed of between 4,200 and 4,700 revolutions per minute to generate an output of about 190 DIN horsepower (over 200 SAE horsepower). This increased the performance of the 3-liter diesel engine by about 2.5 times, from 80 to 190 horsepower. Torque was 275 pounds/feet (38 meters/kilogram) at 3,600 revolutions per minute. In emission and fuel consumption this special engine with a 2.17 fifth gear ratio did not differ significantly from the standard production unit. Acceleration to a speed of 100 kilometers per hour was 6.5 seconds, quite remarkable for this 1,300 kilogram (2,860 pound) vehicle. Average fuel consumption on the record run was 19.8 liters per 100 kilometers, or 11.9 miles per gallon, and oil consumption was 0.7 liters per 1,000 kilometers.

The speeds achieved for the three world's records were for:

5,000 miles	252.540 kmh (156.928 mph)
10,000 kilometers	252.249 kmh (156.748 mph)
10,000 miles	251.798 kmh (156.467 mph)

For the category A, group III, class 8, the record speeds were as follows:

10 kilometers	224.971 kmh	(139.797 mph)
10 miles	231.126 kmh	(143.622 mph)
100 kilometers	251.752 kmh	(156.439 mph)
100 miles	253.676 kmh	(157.634 mph)
500 kilometers	254.755 kmh	(158.305 mph)
500 miles	252.930 kmh	(157.171 mph)
1,000 kilometers	253.307 kmh	(157.405 mph)
1,000 miles	252.737 kmh	(157.051 mph)
5,000 kilometers	252.905 kmh	(157.155 mph)
1 hour	254.856 kmh	(158.368 mph)
6 hours	252.855 kmh	(157.124 mph)
12 hours	253.616 kmh	(157.597 mph)
24 hours	253.030 kmh	(157.233 mph)

Just how much this successful record effort would encourage the engineers at Daimler-Benz to develop an exhaust gas turbocharged diesel engine for their passenger cars was easy to assess, and it seemed quite reasonable to assume that such an automobile was in the not too distant future. Engines used by practically all manufactureres of large trucks—including Mercedes-Benz trucks—were turbocharged diesel units and their reliability and economy were well proven. No adverse effect on engine life and no problems with bearings, gaskets, or other engine parts because of greater stresses had been noticed. Turbocharged diesel engines were definitely believed to be the coming power units for passenger automobiles, for they offered increased horsepower over the normally aspirated engines which seemingly had reached their ultimate in practical size and weight.

The 300SD, a turbocharged diesel sedan, was introduced to the public at the Frankfurt Automobile Show in September 1977.

In 1977, after the development work on the turbocharged diesel passenger car was finished, Daimler-Benz engineers believed that they could improve considerably on the records established by the diesel-powered experimental vehicle the previous year.

After considerable modifications to the test vehicle and engine they went in late April 1978 again to the 12.64 kilometer long SASN test track at Nardo in southern Italy. Initial testing had been carried out in February of that year.

Above: **The C111 ready to go again on the track.**
Below: **The C111 on the track at Nardo, Italy**

Above: The improved
C111/III for the 1978 record
attempt. *Left:* The Mark III
with airholes for cooling
of rear brakes.

A vastly altered, highly streamlined body with a very low drag coefficient of 0.195—modern cars have 0.4 to 0.45—had been designed for the experimental C111 vehicle, and the five-cylinder turbocharged 3-liter diesel engine with a compressor intercooler was developed to produce an amazing 230 DIN (170 kilowatt) horsepower. Turbo boost pressure was increased from 24 to 30 pounds per square inch (psi) to reach that power.

The C111 Mark III vehicle, constructed to travel safely at a constant speed of over 300 kilometers (186 miles) per hour, had an elongated front end. The wheels were entirely enclosed by the long aerodynamic body of fiberglass with carbonfiber reinforcing. The headlights were placed behind clear fairings. A single, tall rear vertical tail was to insure high speed stability. The overall length was 211.8 inches, width 67.5 inches, and height 41.1 inches, front track 49.6 inches and rear track 52 inches. The 107.1-inch wheelbase vehicle weighed 1,348 kilograms (2,965 pounds). Dunlop tires were mounted on 8-inch rims with 9.5-inch in the rear.

The five-cylinder diesel engine had a Garret AiResearch turbocharger unit and displacing 2,999 cubic centimeters (183 cubic inches) developed 230 DIN horsepower at 4,400 to 4,600 revolutions per minute. Compression was lowered to 17:1 from the usual 21.5:1. Torque was 296 pounds/feet at 3,600 revolutions per minute. A ZF 5-speed gear box was used, and the rear axle rate had a final drive ratio of 1.65 to 1. At 4,600 revolutions per minute the speed was 210 miles per hour.

The drivers selected were two of the previous record team, the project engineers Hans Liebold and Guido Moch, and the fine journalists and former long distance drivers Paul Frère of Belgium and Rico Steinmann of Switzerland. And, as on the earlier record attempt, the four drivers would change off when the two 18.5-gallon tanks (140 liters) of fuel became exhausted. The necessary maintenance work was usually completed within 20 to 30 seconds. But the test runs were halted when heavy fog set in and cut the visibility to a dangerous point of about a hundred yards. Still, in twelve hours of driving a distance of 2,345 miles had been covered. Hans Scherenberg was satisfied.

Constant speeds were about 205 miles per hour for the record setting period and the highest average achieved was 199.995 for the 500 kilometer distance. Fuel consumption was most reasonable, just short of 16 liters per 100 kilometers, or 14.75 miles per gallon. Formula I racing cars use about 40 to 60 liters of fuel, have engines of about twice the horsepower, but achieve a maximum speed of about 300 kilometers (186.4 miles) per hour, while the C111/III reached 325 kilometers (205 miles) per hour!

The nine world records set on April 29 and 30, 1978, included some set by gasoline-engined vehicles of considerably larger displacement engines on the Bonneville salt flats. It was a remarkable achievement for a diesel engine to better those excellent times. In addition to these records, eleven international records for land vehicles in category A, group III, class 8 (turbocharged diesel engines with over 2,000 and less than 3,000 cubic centimeter displacement) were also established, under the supervision of the Fédération Internationale Automobile.

The records were as follows:

	New Records	Old Records
100 kilometers	316.484 kmh (196.674 mph)	302.01 kmh (187.66 mph)
100 miles	319.835 kmh (198.736 mph)	306.85 kmh (190.67 mph)
500 kilometers	321.860 kmh (199.995 mph)	294.85 kmh (183.21 mph)
500 miles	320.788 kmh (199.328 mph)	285.22 kmh (177.23 mph)
1,000 kilometers	318.308 kmh (197.787 mph)	285.42 kmh (177.35 mph)
1,000 miles	319.091 kmh (198.274 mph)	278.10 kmh (172.80 mph)
1 hour	321.843 kmh (199.984 mph)	306.87 kmh (190.68 mph)
6 hours	317.796 kmh (197.469 mph)	277.42 kmh (172.38 mph)
12 hours	314.463 kmh (195.398 mph)	273.93 kmh (170.21 mph)

The apprentices ready to compete in the 1977 "Kilometer marathon"

Records for Marathon Mileage Misers

What may well be a record of long duration for the most fuel-efficient vehicle was accomplished when several teams of young apprentices at Daimler-Benz constructed some excitingly exotic vehicles for an economy competition, the "Kilometer Marathon," sponsored by an oil company and a car magazine in Germany, at the Hockenheim Motodrom in 1980.

Urged perhaps by the setting of new speed records by highly sophisticated experts, these set by less experienced factory personnel are of interest. The factory employed now about 6,000 young people who learn a skilled trade in this historic European apprenticeship tradition by working at a company of their choice. Usually, a stimulating project is proposed in their special training sessions and the boys will work on it in small groups under expert technical guidance.

The victorious streamlined vehicle, the Untertürkheim I, driven by 17-year old Volker Schramm, was 17.7 inches high, 116.14 inches long, and ran on bicycle wheels. It was propelled by an air-cooled, one-cylinder Faryman 200-cubic centimeter diesel engine, modified to develop 1 horsepower at 1,000 revolutions per minute. The fully enclosed vehicle of light tubular frame construction with a plastic skin weighed 121 pounds.

The world's fuel economy record set by the vehicle was equal to a consumption of 2,418 miles per gallon (or 1,479.9 kilometers per liter). The two competing Sindelfingen Sparmobiles placed second and third with a rating of 2,041.66 and 1,481.85 miles per gallon, respectively. The second place finisher used a narrow arrow-styled vehicle with a side box to house the other rear wheel.

A year before, the winning average fuel consumption rate was 2,281.58, set by a highly efficient vehicle. That car, incidentally, achieved an even better than 3,000 miles per gallon average during a fuel economy competition in Switzerland in October under ideal conditions.

In a previous contest, the average fuel consumption of the winning vehicle was calculated to be 1,585 miles per gallon (or 1,028 kilometers

The Winner, the "Untertürkheim I," of the economy marathon

The winner, the "three-wheeled cigar," of the 1977 contest

per liter). The second best time, made by a four-wheeled vehicle with a completely streamlined body, reached a calculated 1,470 miles per gallon.

Driving styles were rather unique and quite unsuited for daily traffic because the driver would accelerate his vehicle very slowly to an about 30 miles (50 kilometers) per hour speed, then coast until the speed dropped to about 18 miles (30 kilometers) per hour, then accelerate again for an average speed of 21 kilometers per hour. However, the run was completed within the allowed sixty minutes, actually in about 43, and the average speed of Schramm was 9.3 miles per hour during the seven laps around the 1.3 mile Grand Prix circuit. The driver's seat was suspended within a hammock and the vehicle actually required 45 percent more power without the driver than with him.

Theoretically, a drive in the three-wheeled fuel saving vehicle across the entire United States would consume less than 2 gallons of diesel fuel—but what a way to go!

The C111/III record car, flanked by the two competitors in the economy test

The "Untertürkheim I"

Easy access to the rear seats in the 300CD of 1980

Model 300CD

The 300CD, the coupe with the OM 617 five cylinder diesel engine, was added to the line of cars to be sold in the United States for 1978. The identical W123 body style, first introduced to the public at the 1977 Geneva Auto Show in March, was also available with the fuel-injected 2.8-liter gasoline engine as 280CE, or the 230 gasoline engine as 230C.

The diesel coupe had, of course, all of the features found in the top line, such as four-wheel power disc brakes, automotive transmission, power steering, automotive climate control, central locking system, cruise control, stereo radio, quartz-crystal clock, tinted windshield, fog lights, power windows, six-way adjustable front bucket seats, radial tires, as standard equipment in the United States. By 1980, light-alloy wheels were also furnished as a standard item.

The wheelbase was 106.7 inches (2,710 millimeters), actually 3.3 inches less than that of the 300D sedan, with an overall length of 187.5 inches (4,763 mm). The height was 54.9 inches (1,395 mm). The curb weight of the coupe was 3,495 pounds (1,585 kilograms), but for the 1981 model it was 3,420 pounds, just 10 pounds less than that of the sedan. Steering wheel ratio was 3.2, against the 2.7 for the sedan (again, by 1981 all cars had a 3.2 ratio), and the turning circle was 36.1 feet (11 meters). Gear ratios and rear axle ratio were the same as on the 300D, and maximum speed was 93 miles per hour (150 km/hr). Acceleration for the 0 to 100 kilometers per hour was 20.8 seconds for the 1979 cars, and 19.2 seconds for the 1980 models. All of the 300D models, the sedans, coupes, and station wagons had the same performance, although their weights differed slightly. (Just for comparison, the 280CE, the same bodied coupe with the gasoline engine, needed but 12.9 seconds for the 0-100 km/hr acceleration.)

The coupe definitely had a more sporty feel, and certainly a much more sporty appearance than the sedan, but the main feature was the fantastic economy of the car. The Environmental Protection Agency rated the 300CD for 1979 at 23 miles per gallon for city and 28 mpg for highway driving, or a combined 25 miles per gallon. For 1981, the city driving cycle was rated at 24 miles per gallon.

Front view of the 300CD of 1980

The cost of the 300CD was at the time of introduction, at the east and Gulf coasts, $19,987. By 1979 it was $23,619. In 1980 it was $27,707, and in 1981, $30,314 (east coast).

All engine specifications were identical to those of the other 3-liter diesel units. By 1981, the 183 cubic inch (2,998 cubic centimeter) engine developed 83 SAE horsepower at 4,200 revolutions per minute and had a torque of 120 pounds/feet (16.7 meters/kilogram) at 2,400 revolutions per minute. Rear axle ratio was 3.46:1.

Production of the 300CD model [123] (from May/August 1977)

was in	1977	1,078 units
	1978	2,485 units
	1979	1,834 units
	1980	1,770 units
	total	7,167 units

Above: The 300CD
coupe of 1981. *Left:*
Instrument panel of the
300CD of 1980.

Technical Data

	300CD (W123)
Engine type	5 cyl diesel, overhead camshaft (OM 616)
Bore and stroke	91 x 92.4mm (3.58 x 3.64 in)
Displacement	3005 cc (183.4 cu in); 1979: 2998 cc (183 cu in)
Power output	80 hp (DIN) @ 4000 rpm; 1979: 88 hp (DIN) @ 4400 rpm; U.S. 1977: 77 hp (SAE) @ 4000 rpm; 1980: 83 hp (SAE) @ 4200 rpm
Compression ratio	21:1
Torque	17.5 mkg @ 2400 rpm (126.6 ft/lb); 1979: 17.5 mkg @ 2400 rpm; U.S. 1977: 15.9 mkg (110.0 ft/lb); U.S. 1980: 16.7 mkg @ 2400 rpm (120 ft/lb)
Fuel injection	Bosch five plunger pump
Maximum engine speed	5300 rpm; U.S. 1980: 4200 rpm
Engine speed at 100 km/hr	2995 rpm; automatic: 3090 rpm
Gear ratios	I. 3.90:1 automatic: I. 3.98:1 II. 2.30:1 II. 2.39:1 III. 1.41:1 III. 1.46:1 IV. 1.00:1 IV. 1.00:1
Rear axle ratio	3.46
Chassis	unit frame and body
Suspension	independent front and rear, with coil springs; diagonal swing axle, coil springs, anti-lift control, stabilizer bar
Brakes and area	dual circuit discs, power assisted, 278/279mm (10.9/11.0 in)
Wheelbase	2710mm (106.7 in)
Track, front/rear	1488/1446mm (58.6/56.9 in)
Length	4640mm (182.6 in); U.S.: 4763mm (187.5 in)
Width	1786mm (70.3 in)
Height	1395mm (54.9 in)
Tires	175 SR 14; 1979: 195/70 HR 14; U.S.: 195/70 HR 14
Turning circle	11 meters (36.1 ft)
Steering type and ratio	recirculating ball (3.2 turns), servo assisted
Weight	1445 kg (3179 lbs); U.S.: 1585 kg (3487 lbs); U.S.: 1978: 1575 kg (3465 lbs); U.S. 1980: 1545 kg (3399 lbs)
Maximum speed	148 km/hr (92 mph); automatic: 143 km/hr (89 mph); 1979: 155 km/hr; automatic: 150 km/hr (93 mph)
Acceleration	19.9 sec 0–100 km/hr; automatic: 20.8 sec; 1979: 17.8 sec; automatic: 19.2 sec
Fuel consumption	10.8 liters/100 km (21.5 mpg); 1979: at 120 km/hr: 11.5 liters; automatic: 12.4 liters
Fuel tank capacity	80 liters (21.1 gallons)

Front view of the 300SD of 1979

Model 300SD

At the time of the introduction of the 300SD at the Frankfurt Automobile Show in 1977, Joachim Zahn, chairman of the Board of Management of Daimler-Benz, stated that "with the start of series production of the turbodiesel a piece of new territory has been opened up, not only as regards performance, economy, and environmental compatibility, but also in terms of motive power for vehicles of the upper category in such an important market [that is, the United States]." And Hans Scherenberg, member of the Management Board and Chief of Research and Development at Daimler-Benz, suggested that the "300SD turbocharged diesel is another milestone in the history of the development of passenger cars with diesel engines, which began more than forty years ago at Daimler-Benz with the 260D. The working principle of the diesel engine does not permit an increase of specific output by raising the engine speed as in the spark-ignition engine. We have already made use to a large degree of the possibility of boosting output by enlarging the swept volume. The most recent example is the first five-cylinder engine in 1974. More than 120,000 of these units have been produced. Rising demands concerning emissions and energy consumption on the one hand led us a number of years ago to study intensively the possibilities of exhaust gas turbocharging in cars, as well. It took extensive development work to obtain sufficient boost pressure in the lower speed ranges and thus high torque for acceleration without, on the other hand, overcharging the engine at high speed. This problem has now been satisfactorily solved in cooperation with turbocharger specialists."

The chief engineer also pointed out that turbocharging had actually a long tradition at the company, having begun in the 1940s with airplane engines, extending to large industrial units, and volume-production of turbocharged engines for trucks. "The 300SD is now the first standard production car equipped with a five-cylinder diesel engine with exhaust gas turbocharger and by-pass control," Hans Scherenberg concluded.

This first passenger automobile powered by a turbocharged diesel engine had the body style of the W116 S-class of cars *(Oberklasse)*, identical to those of the larger displacement gasoline sedans, and was considerably more luxurious than the styles used for the smaller displacement classes of the intermediate line of cars.

The 300SD was scheduled to go into production in April 1978 and to be sold exclusively in the United States market only, at least, until production could be increased to make sufficient cars to satisfy the anticipated great demand everywhere. With the addition of this new luxury model, there were four diesel-engined models available in this country in 1978. The four-cylinder 240D sedan, the five-cylinder 300D sedan, and the five-cylinder 300CD coupe, were the others which incidentally represented over 50 percent of all Mercedes-Benz passenger cars sold in North America that past year.

Rear view of the 300SD with short-lived modernistic insignia

The 300SD sedan of 1978

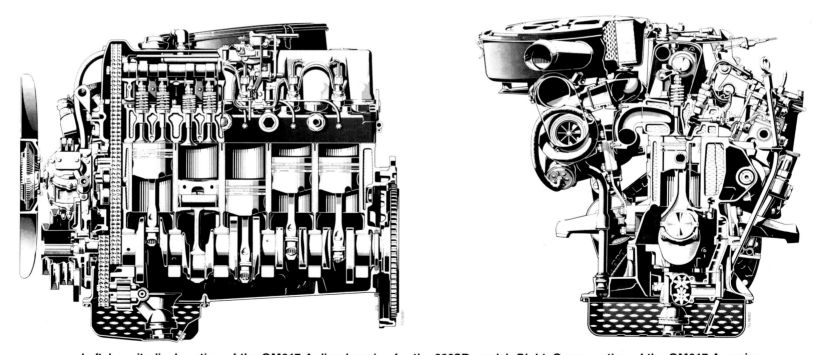

Left: Longitudinal section of the OM617 A diesel engine for the 300SD model. *Right:* Cross section of the OM617 A engine.

Standard equipment on the 300SD models included the automatic transmission, automatic climate control, four-wheel power disc brakes, stereo radio and automatic antenna, central locking system, power windows and power steering, quartz-crystal clock, electrically defrosted rear window, cruise control, and light alloy wheels, among other items.

The 2,998 cubic centimeter (183 cubic inch) displacement OM 617.950 engine with a bore of 90.9 millimeters and 92.4 millimeter stroke, developed 115 (DIN) horsepower (110 SAE) at 4,200 revolutions per minute and torque of 23.2 meters/kilogram (168 pounds/feet) at 2,400 revolutions per minute. It had a 21.5:1 compression ratio, and a five plunger Bosch pump with injection timer. The turbo-charger (TA 0301) was supplied by the Garrett AiResearch corporation and produced 11 pounds per square inch (psi) boost at 2,000 revolutions per minute under full load.

A four-speed automatic transmission was provided. The final drive ratio was 3.07:1 (the 300D had a 3.46:1 ratio). Despite the increase of 44 percent in power (from 80 to 115 horsepower) over the regular five cylinder diesel engine and an increase in torque of 37 percent, fuel consumption was actually 9 percent less!

The body dimensions of the W116 S-class cars were 2,865 millimeter (112.8 inch) wheelbase and 5,220 millimeters (205.5 inches) overall length. Individual front wheel suspension dual control arm, coil springs, gas pressure shock absorbers, anti-dive control and torsion bar stabilizer were provided. The rear axle had the Mercedes-Benz diagonal swing axle, coil springs, gas pressure shock absorbers and torsion bar stabilizer. Curb weight was 1,765 kilograms (3,883 pounds).

Maximum speed was given as 165 kilometers (102.5 miles) per hour. The fuel tank held 82 liters (21.7 gallons) and fuel consumption was rated at 10.6 liters per 100 kilometers, at 68 miles per hour, or about 22 miles per gallon. However, the Environmental Protection Agency, using a quite different and totally unrealistic testing method to determine fuel consumption averages, rated the 300SD for 1979 at 24 miles per gallon for city driving and 29 miles per gallon for the highway cycle, or 26 combined. This would allow for a cruising range of over 560 miles of driving from one tank full of fuel.

For the 1980 model year, the highway figure was even better, up to 32, and the combined fuel consumption rating went up to 27 miles per

Above: **The OM617A diesel turbocharged engine of the 300SD.**
Below: **Injection side of the same engine.**

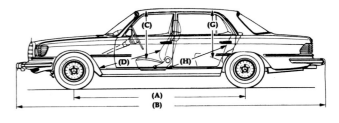

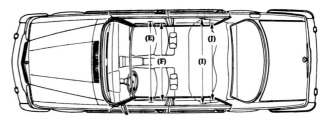

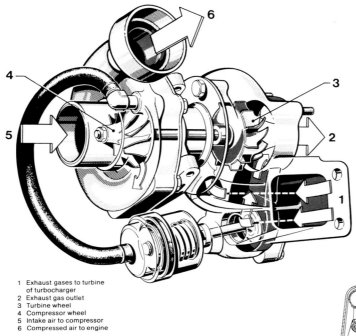

1 Exhaust gases to turbine
  of turbocharger
2 Exhaust gas outlet
3 Turbine wheel
4 Compressor wheel
5 Intake air to compressor
6 Compressed air to engine

Above: Diagram of the
turbocharger for the OM617A
engine. *Right:* Engine detail
showing combustion chamber and
piston cooling of engine.

Interior Dimensions
300 SD

Wheelbase (in./mm.)	(A)	115.6/2935
Overall Length (in./mm.)	(B)	202.6/5145
Head Room Front (in./mm.)	(C)	38.5/979
Leg Room Front (in./mm.)	(D)	41.9/1064
Hip Room Front (in./mm.)	(E)	56.4/1432
Shoulder Room Front (in./mm.)	(F)	56.2/1428
Head Room Rear (in./mm.)	(G)	37.1/943
Leg Room Rear (in./mm.)	(H)	34.4/873
Hip Room Rear (in./mm.)	(I)	57.8/1468
Shoulder Room Rear (in./mm.)	(J)	55.7/1416

Dimensions of the 300SD of 1981

gallon. The California figures were 24 and 31, for a combined rating of 27. For 1981, with the newer body style, the ratings were understandably even better, 26 for city and 30 for highway driving. A tank of fuel was sufficient for 609 miles!

Acceleration for the 1979 300SD model for the 0 to 100 kilometers per hour was 16.2 seconds, and for the 1980 cars 17.0 seconds, more than two seconds faster than that posted by the regular aspirated diesel 300D sedan of 19.2 seconds.

The new body style W126 of the S-class was introduced at the Frankfurt Auto Show in September 1979, but would be available in the United States not until the end of the following year as 1981 models. In Europe the cars went on sale a year earlier. The two new models of this S-class offered in the United States, were the 300SD and the 380SEL only.

In 1979 the 300SD sedan was actually the fastest selling Mercedes-Benz diesel model in this country with 11,067 units being sold. It beat the second best selling model, the 240D, by merely 1 (one) unit. That year, diesel-engined passenger cars accounted for 67.4 percent of the total Mercedes-Benz passenger cars being sold in the United States.

Production of the 300SD, from early 1977 until the end of 1979 was 19,215 units. The price in the United States was in February 1979 $26,265 (east coast), but by January 1980 it had risen to $30,632. (The 1981 model sold for $34,185 (east coast), fully equipped, although there were some optional items such as the electric sunroof at $795, metallic paint at $778, and leather upholstery at $1,078.)

Introduced under the motto "Engineered for the Future—to meet the Demands of Today," the new line of S-class cars had brand new, lighter 380SE and 500SE gasoline engines and considerably altered bodies, for a combined saving of as much as up to 280 kilograms (616 pounds) in total weight over the previous models.

Actually, development work on these new W126 types had begun seven years before when the main emphasis was on emission controls and safety standards. The economic factor was then not a dominating concern, as it was to become at the time of introduction of these new models in 1979. Yet, an overall saving in fuel of approximately 10 percent was achieved in the new gasoline models.

The 300SD shared, of course, the body style of this *Oberklasse* (upper class) of cars. They had a lower, smoother hood line and were

Above: **The 300SD model of 1979.** *Below:* **Passenger compartment of the 300SD sedan, 1979.**

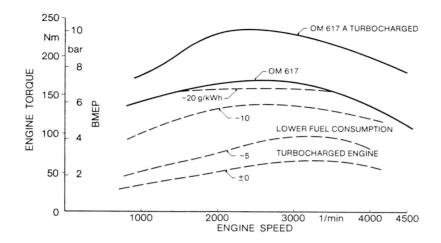

Comparison chart for the diesel engines

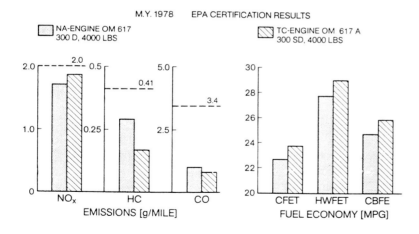

M.Y. 1978   EPA CERTIFICATION RESULTS

☐ NA-ENGINE OM 617
    300 D, 4000 LBS

▨ TC-ENGINE OM 617 A
    300 SD, 4000 LBS

**Comparison chart for the 300D and 300SD diesel engine
in emission and fuel economy**

lighter (by as much as 176 pounds) than the style they replaced. They were actually 3.5 centimeters (1.38 inches) longer and 5.0 centimeters (1.97 inches) narrower. The drag coefficient was an astounding 0.36, an improvement of about 14 percent. The redesigned front end did not sacrifice seat height, door height, interior width, or the view of all four corners of the car by the driver. Square halogen sealed beam headlights replaced the former round type. Windshield wipers were recessed for a cleaner look and the rear windows had a greater slope than before. The hood and deck lid were of aluminum, saving about 42 pounds. And high strength steel was used for weight-saving whenever possible, resulting in even stronger sections of the basic structure, yet also improving safety and durability. A redesigned, cleaner looking bumper of fiberglass, plastic, and aluminum was used for greater strength and lighter weight.

The climate control system was electronically instead of vacuum operated for simplification and improvement. Two outside mirrors, one for each side, electrically controlled from the console, were provided, as was a center sun visor. These were some of the additional interior refinements found in the new style bodies.

The 2,998 cubic centimeter five-cylinder turbocharged diesel engine developed now 120 SAE horsepower at 4,350 revolutions per minute and had a torque of 170 pounds/feet (23.6 meters/kilograms) at 2,400 revolutions per minute. A new, light-weight four-speed automatic transmission for smoother shifting was made available for the new model.

The turbocharged diesel engine was considered the very ultimate development in diesel engine design, and therefore it may be of interest to show graphically the technical data of all of the diesel passenger cars manufactured over the years by Daimler-Benz. The several graphs show a tremendous improvement in practically every field.

Production of the 300SD model [116] (from February 1977 until September 1980) was in

	1977	51 units
	1978	5,970 units
	1979	13,194 units
	1980	9,419 units
total		28,634 units

Production of the 300SD model [126] (from September 1979) was in

	1979	3 units
	1980	4,857 units
total		4,860 units

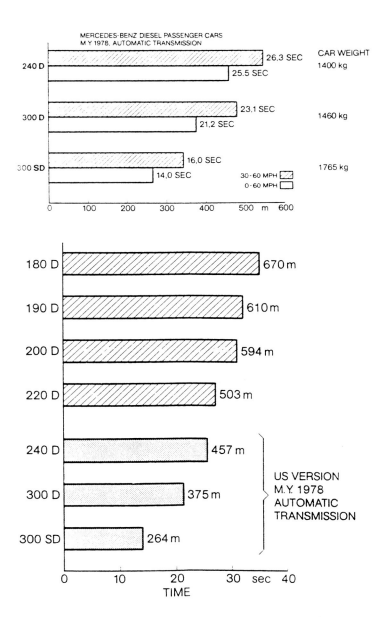

Acceleration comparison chart for all diesel engines

TYP		ENGINE	PRODUCTION YEAR	DISPLACEMENT cm³	STROKE mm	BORE mm	MAX. OUTPUT AT SPEED (DIN) kW	1/min	TORQUE AT SPEED Nm	1/min	NUMBER OF CYLINDERS	DRY ENGINE WEIGHT KG
260D		OM138	1936	2545	100	90	33	3300			4	
170D		OM636	1949	1697	100	73,5	28	3200	96	2000	4	
180D		OM636	1953	1767	100	75	31	3500	101	2000	4	
190D		OM621	1958	1897	83,6	85	37	4000	108	2200	4	
200D		OM621	1965	1988	83,6	87	40	4200	113	2400	4	
200D		OM615	1967	1988	83,6	87	40	4200	113	2400	4	
220D		OM615	1967	2197	92,4	87	44	4200	126	2400	4	
240D		OM616	1973	2404	92,4	91	48	4200	137	2400	4	
300D		OM617	1974	3005	92,4	91	59	4000	172	2400	5	
200D		OM615	1976										195
220D		OM615	1976										197
240D		OM616	1976	AS ABOVE									197
300D		OM617	1976										229
300CD		OM617	1977										229
300SD		OM 617 A	1978	2998	92,4	90,9	85	4200	235	2400	5 TURBO-CHARGED		244

Chart of *all* diesel engine types built by Daimler-Benz for passenger cars

123

The 300SD sedan of 1981, U.S. version

Technical Data

	300SD *(W116)*	300SD *(W126)*
Engine type	5 cyl diesel, overhead camshaft, with turbo-charger (OM 617A)	5 cyl diesel, overhead camshaft, with turbo-charger (OM 617A)
Bore and stroke	90.9 x 92.4mm (3.58 x 3.64 in)	91 x 92.4mm (3.58 x 3.64 in)
Displacement	2998 cc (182.9 cu in)	2998 cc (182.9 cu in)
Power output	115 hp (DIN) @ 4200 (110 SAE hp); U.S. 1980: 120 hp (SAE) @ 4350 rpm	125 hp (DIN); U.S.: 120 hp (SAE)
Compression ratio	21.5:1	21.5:1
Torque	23.2 mkg @ 2400 rpm (168 ft/lb); U.S. 1980: 23.6 mkg @ 2400 rpm (170 ft/lb)	25.5 mkg @ 2400 rpm U.S.: 23.6 mkg (170 ft/lb) @ 2400 rpm
Maximum engine speed	4350 rpm	5100 rpm; U.S.: 4350 rpm
Fuel injection	Bosch five plunger pump with injection timer	Bosch five plunger pump with injection timer
Engine speed at 100 km/hr	2580 rpm	
Gear ratios	automatic, standard: I. 3.98:1 II. 2.39:1 III. 1.46:1 IV. 1.00:1	I. 3.90:1 II. 2.30:1 III. 1.41:1 IV. 1.00:1
Rear axle ratio	3.07	3.07
Chassis	unit frame and body	unit frame and body
Suspension	independent front and rear, coil springs, anti-roll bar; diagonal swing axle, coil springs, anti-roll bar, standard level control	independent front and rear, coil springs; diagonal swing axle, coil springs, anti-roll bar, level control standard
Brakes and area	dual circuit discs, power assisted, brake pad wear indicator, 278/279mm (10.9/11.0 in)	dual circuit discs, power assisted, brake pad wear indicator, 278/279mm (10.9/11.0 in)
Wheelbase	2865mm (112.8 in)	2935mm (115.6 in)
Track, front/rear	1521/1505mm (59.9/59.3 in)	1545/1517mm (60.8/59.7 in)
Length	5220mm (205.5 in)	4995mm (196.6 in); U.S.: 5145mm (202.6 in)
Width	1870mm (73.6 in)	1820mm (71.6 in)
Height	1425mm (56.1 in)	1430mm (56.3 in)
Tires	185 HR 14	195/70 RS 14
Turning circle	11.59 meters (38 feet)	11.80 meters (38.7 ft)
Steering type and ratio	recirculating ball (2.7 turns); servo assisted	recirculating ball (2.7 turns); servo assisted
Weight	1765 kg (3883 lbs); U.S.: 1745 kg (3839 lbs); 1980: 1715 kg (3773 lbs)	1705 kg (3751 lbs)
Maximum speed	165 km/hr (103 mph)	165 km/hr (103 mph) automatic
Acceleration	12.7 sec 0–100 km/hr	15 sec 0–100 km/hr
Fuel consumption	10.6 liters/100 km (22 mph)	11.1 liters at 120 km/hr
Fuel tank capacity	82 liters (21.7 gallons)	77 liters (20.3 gallons)

The 300TD station wagon of 1977

Models 240TD and 300TD

A brand new line of station wagons was introduced at the Frankfurt Auto Show in 1977, "opening up for Mercedes-Benz the increasingly important market for recreation and tourism," as the chief engineer stated in his presentation talk.

The "Touristik und Transport—tourist and transport" wagons were scheduled to be built at the factory in Bremen, beginning in April 1978. Although station wagons had been available on a Mercedes chassis by several body builders, this was the first one manufactured by Daimler-Benz itself. The "T" models were, as the cross-country vehicles before them, available with five different engines and virtually any combination of loading possibilities.

Three of the engines used were the gasoline types, the 230, 250, and 280E, and two the diesel types, the four-cylinder 240D of 65 DIN horsepower, and the five-cylinder 300D of 80 DIN horsepower. Basically the 123 body was utilized. The roof line was harmoniously integrated into the body style, retaining the sedan character, but at the same time increasing the storage space dramatically. In fact, the station wagons performed as well as the similarly powered sedans, and were as comfortable. All of those special features were also standard equipment on the wagons.

The wheelbase was 2,795 millimeters (110.0 inches) and the overall length of the wagons was 4,725 millimeters (186.0 inches). Width was 1,786 millimeters (70.3 inches) and height was 1,425 millimeters (56.1 inches), and with roof railing 1,470 millimeters. The weight of the 240TD was 1,485 kilograms (3,267 pounds) and that of the 300TD was 1,545 kilograms (3,399 pounds).

For the United States the 300TD, in the 1980 model year, had an overall length of 190.9 inches (4,848 millimeters) and weight of 3,605 pounds (1,635 kilograms). Maximum speed for the 240TD was, with manual transmission, 138 kilometers (86 miles) per hour, and with the automatic transmission, 133 kilometers (82.6 miles) per hour. The 300TD had a top speed of 148 kilometers (92 miles) and 143 kilometers (89 miles) per hour, respectively.

Above: The rear deck lid open, showing available space
Below: The same, but with even more space (1981 model)

The same 300TD, but other side

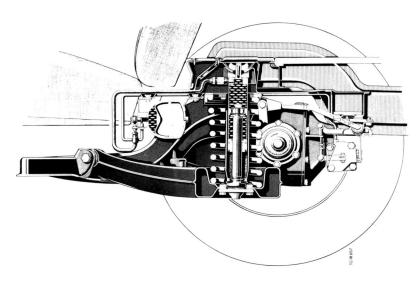

Hydraulic self-leveling device for the 300TD

The hydropneumatic self-leveling device allowed loads of 560 kilograms (1,232 pounds), or with an optional version, 700 kilograms (1.540 pounds). Roof rails for special luggage containers and a vast selection of specific equipment to accommodate practically any imaginable load was made available. The station wagons were indeed usable for a truly immense variety of special purpose hauling.

The rear-end door opened upwards by means of pressurized gas cylinders through a wide angle and gave easy access to the standard loading platform of 1.23 meters length and 1.48 meters width. By folding down the rear bench seat, the platform was extended to 1.78 meters and even 2.03 meters (6.7 feet). Total cargo volume was 73.85 cubic feet.

In the United States, the 300TD was the only model offered for sale, beginning in March 1978. It shared many components with the 300D sedan, such as drive train, front suspension, some body components, and inside trim, and the performance was consequently just as similar.

The five-cylinder diesel engine of 77 SAE horsepower gave the station wagon an Environmental Protection Agency rating of 23 miles

per gallon for city and 28 miles per gallon highway driving. The 18.5 gallon fuel tank thus sufficed for 518 miles of highway driving for this economical 300TD model. For 1981 the ratings were 24 for city and 28 for highway driving. And the tank held now 21.1 gallons, good for 590.8 miles.

Production of the 300TD during 1978 and 1979 was 14,325 units (1 was built in 1977), while during that time a total of 9,390 of the 240TD models were manufactured. The price of the 300TD was early in 1979 $23,900 (east coast), and early in 1980 $28,056, with automatic transmission of course. It was the only kind available in the North American market. In 1977 the 240TD wagon sold for DM 25,052.70, in 1979 for DM 27,193.60, and in 1980 the price was DM 28,159.60. The larger-engined 300TD sold in 1977 for DM 27,317.10, in 1979 for DM 29,265.60, and in 1980 for DM 30,736.

The new 300TD, the turbo-charged diesel engined station wagon, was first introduced at the 1979 Frankfurt Auto Show. This latest variation of the popular line of five different T models would use about ten percent less fuel than the regular 300TD and in addition give better

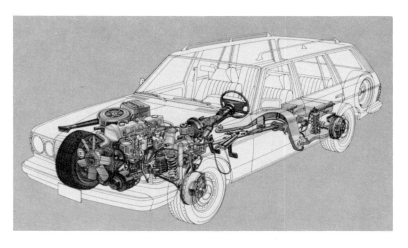

Schematic drawing of the station wagon

The 300TD of 1978 in U.S. trim

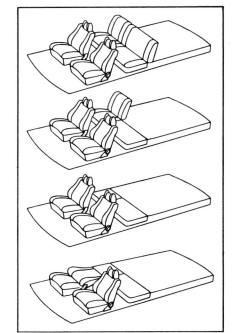

Drawing showing the different carrying spaces available

The 300TD, suitable for a vast variety of purposes

performance. The engine type, the same as that used in the 300SD sedan, developed 122 DIN (120 SAE) horsepower at 4,350 revolutions per minute, and had a maximum torque of 23.6 meters/kilogram (170 pounds/feet) at 2,400 revolutions per minute. (These specifications were for the 1981 model year in the United States).

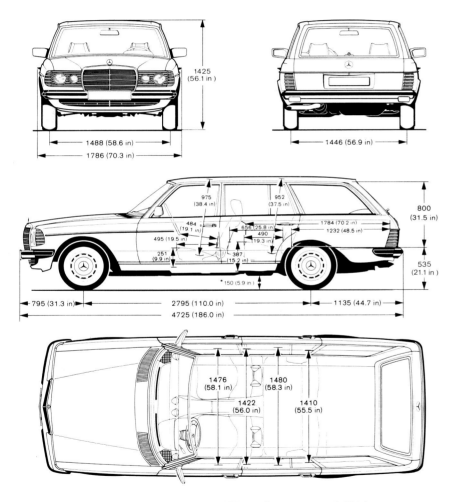

Dimensions of the 300TD station wagon of 1981

Production of this 300TD—designated then as the 300TDT on the factory production program—was scheduled to begin by the middle of 1980. Actually, two such station wagons were built in November and December 1979 and five units in April.

In the United States this was the only station wagon model offered for the 1981 registration year. The turbocharged diesel engine was the identical power plant of the 300SD sedan, now in the new W126 body style, of course.

In addition to the five gasoline-engined models, the 280E sedan, the 280CE coupe, the 380SEL sedan, the 380SL roadster and coupe, and the 380SLC coupe, actually five diesel-engined models were available in the North American market, the 240D sedan, the 300D sedan, the 300CD coupe, the 300SD sedan, and the 300TD wagon.

The main reason for this wide selection of diesel models was not only the decided buyer's preference for this so very economical type, but also the fact that the "corporate average fuel economy" (CAFE) government mandate stipulated a fleet average fuel consumption of 27.5 miles per gallon by the 1985 model year. With the fuel efficient diesel models this goal could be achieved and still the more powerful Mercedes-Benz luxury models could be sold in this country.

In 1980 the 300TD turbodiesel wagon sold for DM 36,521.60.

The Environmental Protection Agency rated the 300TD, as the 300SD sedan, at 26 miles per gallon for city and at 30 miles per gallon for highway driving, giving the wagon a radius of 609 miles from one 20.3-gallon tank of fuel oil.

The 300TD station wagon sold in 1981 for $31,373 (east coast).

Production of the 240TD model [123] (from February 1978)

was in	1978	3,003 units
	1979	6,387 units
	1980	5,820 units
	total	15,210 units

Production of the 300TD model [123] (from September 1977/February 1978)

was in	1977	1 unit
	1978	3,144 units
	1979	11,180 units
	1980	7,523 units
	total	21,848 units

Production of the 300TDT model [123] (from November 1979/April 1980)

was in	1979	2 units
	1980	1,852 units
	total	1,854 units

Technical Data

	240TD *(W123)*	300TD *(W123)*	300TD (turbo) *(W123)*
Engine type	4 cyl diesel, overhead camshaft (OM 616)	5 cyl diesel, overhead camshaft (OM 617)	5 cyl diesel, overhead camshaft, with turbo-charger (OM 617A)
Bore and stroke	91 x 92.4mm (3.58 x 3.64 in) 1979: 90.9 x 92.4mm	91 x 92.4mm (3.58 x 3.65 in) 1979: 90.9 x 92.4mm	91 x 92.4mm (3.58 x 3.64 in)
Displacement	2404 cc (146.7 cu in) 1979: 2399 cc (146.4 cu in)	3005 cc (183.4 cu in) 1979: 2998 cc (183 cu in)	2998 cc (182.9 cu in)
Power output	65 hp (DIN) @ 4200 rpm 1979: 72 hp @ 4400 rpm	80 hp (DIN) @ 4000 rpm 1979: 88 hp @ 4400 rpm; U.S.: 77 hp SAE @ 4000 rpm U.S. 1980: 83 hp (SAE) @ 4200 rpm	125 hp (DIN) @ 4350 rpm U.S.: 120 hp (SAE)
Compression ratio	21:1	21:1	21.5:1
Torque	14 mkg @ 2400 rpm (101.3 ft/lb) 1979: 13.9 mkg @ 2400 rpm	17.5 mkg @ 2400 rpm (126.6 ft/lb) 1979: 17.5 mkg @ 2400 rpm U.S.: 15.9 mkg (115 ft/lb); U.S. 1980: 16.7 mkg @ 2400 rpm (120 ft/lb)	25.5 mkg @ 2400 rpm U.S.: 23.6 mkg (170 ft/lb)
Fuel injection	Bosch four plunger pump	Bosch five plunger pump	Bosch five plunger pump w/injection timer
Maximum engine speed	5300 rpm	5300 rpm; U.S.: 4350 rpm U.S. 1980: 4200 rpm	5100 rpm; U.S.: 4350 rpm
Gear ratios	I. 3.90:1 automatic: I. 3.98:1 II. 2.30:1 II. 2.39:1 III. 1.41:1 III. 1.46:1 IV. 1.00:1 IV. 1.00:1	I. 3.90:1 automatic: I. 3.98:1 II. 2.30:1 II. 2.39:1 III. 1.41:1 III. 1.46:1 IV. 1.00:1 IV. 1.00:1	I. 3.90:1 II. 2.30:1 III. 1.41:1 IV. 1.00:1
Rear axle ratio	3.69	3.46	3.07
Chassis	unit frame and body	unit frame and body	unit frame and body
Suspension	independent front and rear, coil springs; diagonal swing axle, coil springs, torsion bar stabilizer, standard level control	independent front and rear, coil springs; diagonal swing axle, coil springs, torsion bar stabilizer, standard level control	independent front and rear, coil springs; diagonal swing axle, coil springs, torsion bar stabilizer, standard level control
Brakes and area	dual circuit discs, front brake pad wear indicator, 278/279mm (10.9/11.0 in)	dual circuit discs, front brake pad wear indicator, 278/279mm (10.9/11.0 in)	dual circuit discs, front brake pad wear indicator, 278/279mm (10.9/11.0 in)

Rear view of the turbocharged 300TD

	240TD *(W123)*	300TD *(W123)*	300TD (turbo) *(W123)*
Wheelbase	2795mm (110.0 in)	2795mm (110.0 in)	2795mm (110.0 in)
Track, front/rear	1488/1453mm (58.6/57.2 in)	1488/1453mm (58.6/57.2 in)	1488/1453mm (58.6/57.2 in)
Length	4725mm (186.0 in)	4725mm (186.0 in) U.S.: 4848mm (190.9 in)	4725mm (186.0 in) U.S.: 4848mm (190.9 in)
Width	1786mm (70.3 in)	1786mm (70.3 in)	1786mm (70.3 in)
Height	1425mm (56.1 in) 1979: 1470mm (57.9 in)	1425mm (56.1); 1979: 1470mm (57.9 in)	1470mm (57.9 in)
Tires	195 SR 14	195 SR 14	195/70 SR 14
Turning circle	11.29 meters (37 ft)	11.29 meters (37 ft)	11.29 meters (37 ft)
Steering type and ratio	recirculating ball (3.2 turns), power assisted	recirculating ball (3.2 turns), power assisted	recirculating ball (3.2 turns), power assisted
Weight	1485 kg (3267 lbs) 1979: 1505 kg (3311 lbs)	1545 kg (3399 lbs); 1979: 1565 kg (3443 lbs); U.S.: 1715 kg (3773 lbs) U.S. 1980: 1635 kg (3597 lbs)	1610 kg (3542 lbs) U.S.: 1695 kg (3729 lbs)
Maximum speed	138 km/hr (86 mph) automatic: 133 km/hr (83 mph) 1979: 143 km/hr; automatic: 138 km/hr	148 km/hr (92 mph) automatic: 143 km/hr (89 mph) 1979: 155 km/hr; automatic: 150 km/hr	automatic: 165 km/hr (103 mph)
Acceleration	24.6 sec 0–100 km/hr automatic: 27.4 sec 1979: 23.2 sec; automatic: 26.1 sec	19.9 sec 0–100 km/hr; automatic: 20.8 sec 1979: 18.9 sec; automatic: 20.4 sec	automatic: 15 sec 0–100 km/hr
Fuel consumption	9.5 liters/100 km (24.75 mpg) 1979: at 120 km/hr — 11.0 liters; automatic: 11.6	10.8 liters/100 km (21.5 mpg) 1979: at 120 km/hr: 11.3 liters; automatic: 13.0	at 120 km/hr: 11.1 liters
Fuel tank capacity	70 liters (18.5 gallons)	70 liters (18.5 gallons)	70 liters (18.5 gallons)

The turbocharged OM617A diesel engine of the 300TD

The canvas-top version of the Cross-country vehicle

The GD Vehicles

An entirely different line of vehicles—the *Geländewagen,* or cross-country cars—were first shown in 1978. Built by a newly formed joint company of Daimler-Benz and Steyr-Daimler-Puch, the vehicles were manufactured in the new Austrian S-D-P factory.

The whole range—W123—consisted of two basic sizes, the 2,400 millimeter (94.5 inch) and the 2,850 millimeter (112 inch) wheelbase. Three body styles were available, the canvas top, the van, and the station wagon, all with either 4-wheel or with 2-wheel drive. And five different engines were offered. The two diesel versions installed were in the 240GD and the 300GD models, with the proven OM 616 four cylinder and the OM 617 five cylinder engines, as used in the regular sedans. There were no appreciative specification differences in these diesel engines from other types of vehicles.

The major construction components of the cross-country line were taken from the readily available production range of the various Daimler-Benz factories, with certain alterations, of course. Thus, the fully synchronized gear boxes, fitted to the cross-country cars, were identical with those produced by the Bremen factory for their line of light commercial vehicles. And the four-speed automatic transmissions were those used in the Düsseldorf plant for the truck assembly. As fully expected, Daimler-Benz quality was rigidly controlled in the assembly of these utilitarian vehicles.

These versatile cars were excellent on the most difficult terrain, yet could be driven with considerable comfort on paved city streets as well. None were being offered for sale in the United States market, mainly because of the limited production facilities of the new manufacturing enterprise. However, a marketing survey had been conducted in this country to ascertain the demand for such a vehicle. Thus far, no decision had been reached.

**The four different model types
of the Cross-country vehicle**

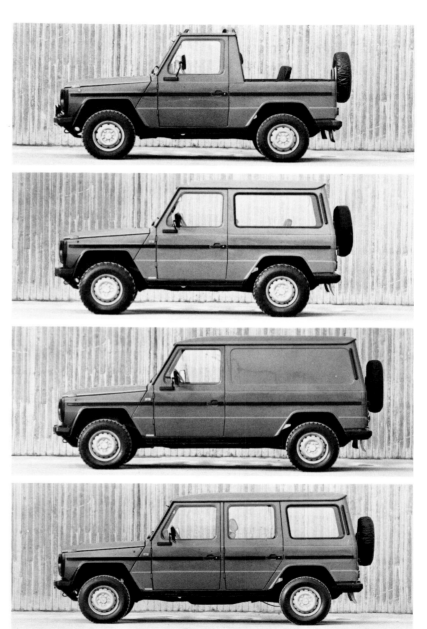

The sturdy chassis, suggesting the
solid construction of the vehicles

The station wagon version of the G-type vehicles

Principles of the Diesel Engine

In presenting this chapter on the operating principle of the diesel engine, we have relied on a paper given by a Daimler-Benz engineer in December 1974, at the introduction of the 300D model. A detailed outline of the basic features and of the main differences between both engine types might prove helpful because most of us have grown up with the gasoline engine as prime power unit for a passenger automobile.

The main characteristics in the combustion principle of the gasoline engine, sometimes also called Otto engine or spark-ignited (SI) engine, are that through the intake a gasoline engine generally aspirates a mixture of fuel and air in a more or less narrow ratio. The output of the engine is controlled by controlling the amount of fuel-air mixture with the throttle. During the compression stroke this fuel-air mixture is compressed at the ratio of about 8-10 to one. Towards the end of the compression the mixture is ignited by an external ignition source via the spark plug. In order to facilitate a good distribution of the fuel within the air and a reliable ignition, the fuel used in a gasoline engine must be introduced fairly early to have enough time for at least partial evaporation.

In contrast to the gasoline engine a diesel engine aspirates pure air, and generally there is no throttle. In other words, the diesel engine always aspirates the maximum of air it can get, in fact, more than it requires for combustion. It operates at air excess. The air is then compressed much higher than in case of the gasoline engine, for example at a ratio of 20-22 to one for a passenger car diesel engine. Some large diesel engines for trucks and ships have a compression ratio of about 14-18 to one. The high compression in a diesel engine results, of course, in a higher pressure and temperature level. Near the

end of the compression, fuel is injected into the cylinder by means of a nozzle, which atomizes the fuel and sprays it into the hot air. The fuel droplets then ignite by themselves, or create self-ignition. There is no external ignition source, and this is, of course, one of the merits of the diesel engine. The output is simply controlled by controlling the amount of fuel injected.

After this very simple comparison of the operating principles of both engine types, we are ready for comparing them somewhat more in depth in a number of categories.

Fuel of high volatility, as used in the gasoline engine, is a fuel which will evaporate readily. The vapor can be ignited by the spark. On the other hand, the diesel engine operates with fuel of very low volatility, which will, in fact, not burn unless it is atomized very carefully and brought into the air of high temperature.

The gasoline engine requires the fuel feed at an early stage, already noted. Most commonly, the inlet air flow is accelerated in the venturi of a carburetor and the fuel is carried along. In case of electronic or similar gasoline injection systems, fuel is injected somewhere into the inlet manifold, but always upstream of the inlet valve. And even in some rare direct gasoline injection systems the fuel is injected directly into the combustion chamber, but again early. All of this is so because gasoline fuel requires time to evaporate thoroughly, mix with the air and get ready for burning. Since fuel feed occurs early, during the intake or very early compression stroke, the feed systems are always of the low pressure type.

Diesel fuel is injected late, towards the end of the compression stroke, generally briefly before top dead center of the piston. Temperature and pressure of the compressed air, due to the high compression

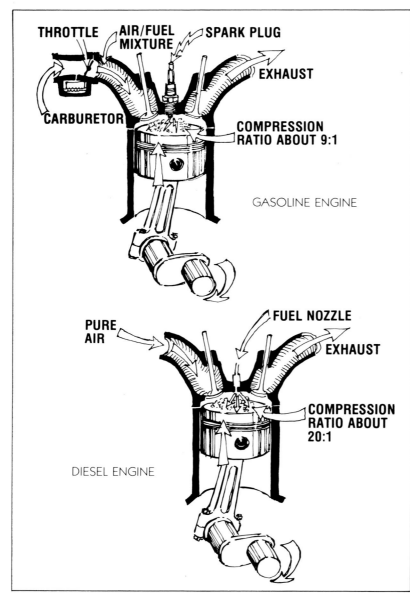

Differences between a gasoline and a diesel engine

ratio of diesel engines, are quite high at that time, around 35 to 45 atmospheres. If one desires to obtain a good penetration of the fuel into the air, and a good atomization and distribution, then the velocity of the fuel droplets has to be high. This is achieved with injection pressures in the order of 200-350 atmospheres, measured in the fuel line in front of the nozzle. Diesel injection systems are, for these reasons, always high pressure injection systems. The resulting peak gas pressures in the combustion chamber amount to 55-75 atmospheres.

The higher the compression ratio, the higher is the thermal efficiency of an engine.

Thermal efficiency is a measure for the quality of formation of mechanical energy from a given chemical energy contained in the fuel. If the thermal efficiency is 40 percent, then that percentage of the fuel's energy is turned into work, and the rest, 60 percent, is wasted.

The air-fuel ratio is a very interesting point. First we have to define the so-called stoichiometric ratio. In order to completely burn a given amount of fuel, a certain definite amount of air is necessary. It can be calculated that one pound of fuel requires about fourteen pounds of air

Category	ENGINE TYPE	
	Gasoline (SI-engine)	Diesel (CI-engine)
Inventor	Nikolaus A. Otto (1832 - 1891)	Rudolf Diesel (1857 - 1913)
Fuel	high volatility	low volatility
Fuel Feed	early (in case of injection: low pressure)	late (always injected, high pressure injection)
Inlet	air/fuel mixture	air only
Compression Ratio	of mixture 8 - 10	of air 14 - 22
Peak Temperature and Pressure	medium (35 - 45 atm) (514.5 - 661.5 psi)	high (55 - 75 atm) (808.5 - 955.5 psi)
Ignition	spark	self
Air/Fuel Ratio	stoichiometric ± 20%	lean + 30% to 600%
Mixture	generally fairly homogeneous	fairly stratified due to concentrated late injection
Load Control	by throttle, controlling amount of mixture (quantity control)	by controlling amount of injected fuel (quality control)

Comparison of characteristics of gasoline and diesel engines

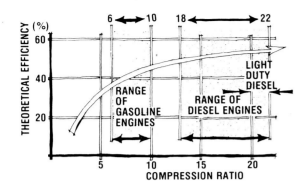

Theoretical efficiency of ideal engine as a function of compression ratio (stoichiometric air/fuel ratio)

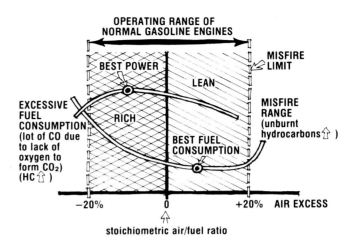

Operating range of normal gasoline engines

for complete combustion. At this stoichiometric ratio each molecule of hydrocarbons in the fuel can find enough molecules of oxygen to burn. Theoretically no fuel or air is left over.

Combustion is complete only if the general conditions are ideal: good evaporation of fuel, warm air, enough oxygen, enough ignition energy, sufficient time, no quenching of flame—to name a few important factors.

In practice gasoline engines operate at around this stoichiometric ratio, which means that air is introduced with a fairly narrow tolerance of about 20 percent around the theoretical amount required for complete combustion. If an engine breathes more air than required, it is operating lean (generally at part load), or if it breathes less, it is operating rich (at full load). So-called lean burning engines attempt to shift the misfire limit to 25 percent, 35 percent, or even higher.

In definite contrast to this, the diesel engine always operates lean, with a large air excess, because there is generally no throttle in the intake. At any given engine speed the diesel engine aspirates practically the same. Large quantity of air, and load control is achieved only by changing the amount of injected fuel. At idle, a typical air excess ratio of 600 percent exists, which means that for every pound of fuel not 14 but 84 pounds of air are aspirated.

The inability of the gasoline engine to burn extremely lean mixtures results from the failure to ignite the more or less homogeneous gasoline-fuel mixture with the customary ignition energies (i.e. spark

intensities), or from the failure to continue the combustion right through the charge.

The ability of the diesel engine to burn extremely lean results from the fact that the mixture is much less homogeneous. The fuel is concentrated in the spray of the injector nozzle. It is thus practically a stratified charge engine, and this is particularly true for those diesel engines using auxiliary combustion chambers, as we shall see later. Moreover, the diesel engine, as a self-igniter, creates its own ignition energy by compression.

The fuel system of a diesel engine consists mainly of the injection pump, the governor, the fuel lines, and the nozzles. A governor is, in simple terms, an interpreter between the driver and the fuel pump. It interprets between the desire of the driver for more or less speed as expressed by his action on the gas pedal and the fuel pump, telling it to deliver more or less fuel.

In addition it has an overriding function controlling or governing the engine's idle speed, or the maximum speed, independent of any action by the driver. For example, a simple governor for controlling a desired speed is the centrifugal governor, in which masses on a lever system are moved inwardly and outwardly against a spring force, depending upon the speed of rotation. This basically simple device dates back to

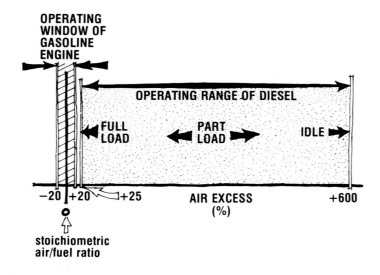

Operating range of diesel engines

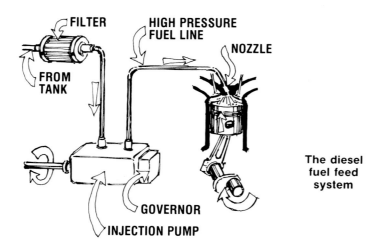

The diesel fuel feed system

James Watt, who invented it for his steam engine. In a diesel engine governor the motion of these masses—over a system of levers—acts on the control rod of the injection pump which defines the quantity of fuel delivered by the pump. Besides this governor (called a mechanical governor) there are other types, for example, the pneumatic governor.

The injection pump is a positive displacement type pump and in its most simple form incorporates one piston or plunger for each cylinder. From there on one delivery or discharge line leads to each injection nozzle. Diesel injection systems have to meter the precisely desired amount of fuel, and they have to do this at the correct time. Since combustion in a self-ingition engine starts upon introduction of the fuel, injection timing in a diesel engine has the function of ignition timing in a gasoline engine. In fact, another device on the injection pump, more or less complicated, varies the injection timing with operating conditions, the so-called timing device. The total unit, injection pump, governor and timing device, is generally maintenance free.

We distinguish between two different basic approaches to diesel combustion, one is the direct injection system, the other is called the indirect injection system.

In the direct injection, the diesel fuel is sprayed directly into the main combustion chamber. The piston may or may not have a recess of a certain configuration.

In the category of indirect injection diesels, the fuel is injected into a small auxiliary chamber, generally located somewhere in the cylinder head.

Today we know of two different indirect injection diesel engines, the swirl chamber and the pre-chamber diesel engine. Combustion in the indirect injection diesel engines proceeds somewhat different than in the direct injection types. Above all it is slower. The differences in design, combustion, heat transfer, and so on, lead to a difference in the features of these systems. Let us examine the most important items in which they differ: fuel consumption, noise, and cold starting capability.

The indirect injection diesel engines are superior in noise level and cold starting features. On the other hand, they have to pay for these advantages by a somewhat reduced efficiency. Their cold starting superiority is due to a simple trick: in the auxiliary chambers a glow plug can be located. These glow plugs are energized before the initial start by running a fairly high current through them. The glowing coil of the plug when red hot will assist the initiation of the first few combustions after the start. The wire is a special high temperature non-corrosive material, and such plugs are maintenance free.

Daimler-Benz selected the pre-chamber system for passenger cars on the ground of its cold start and superior noise features. But the company also actually built and tested experimental direct and swirl chamber diesel engines in the size suitable for passenger cars. With the relatively small cylinder size for such an engine, the minimum temperature for a safe start of a direct injection diesel engine is about 20° Fahrenheit (-5° Celsius), while the pre-chamber has no problems down to -15° Fahrenheit (-25° Celsius).

The differences in combustion noise stem from the different pressure rise rates and peak pressure levels. These are, at full load and 4,000 revolutions per minute: the highest noise level for direct injection (with a pressure rise rate of 8 bars and peak pressure of 90); the medium noise level for the swirl chamber system (with a pressure rise rate of 4 bars and peak pressure of 75); and the lowest noise level for the pre-chamber system (with a pressure rise rate of 2 bars and peak pressure of 60).

To compare the gasoline with the diesel engine, we shall conduct the comparison in a displacement range of slightly over two liters, that means on a large four-cylinder passenger car engine.

The disadvantages of the diesel engine are that it has, relatively speaking, less specific output, that is, less output from the same displacement. A 2.3 liter gasoline engine (European version) develops 100 percent horsepower and 100 percent torque, while the 2.3-liter diesel engine with a hypothetical pre-chamber develops 65 percent horsepower and torque. (The U.S. version of the gasoline engine develops 90 percent horsepower and 95 percent torque, mainly due to the increase in exhaust back pressure because of the catalytic converter.)

The diesel engine requires no emission controls, and the same version can be marketed in the United States and in Europe. Its output and torque are definitely lower. Therefore, on an equal displacement basis the diesel engine will show inferior performance. Yet its weight and first cost will be somewhat higher due to the demand on increased structural stiffness and rigidity based upon the higher peak combustion pressure.

It is, of course, possible to compensate for the diesel engine's inherent relative deficiency in output by increasing its displacement. Then, for identical horsepower output a two-liter gasoline engine would

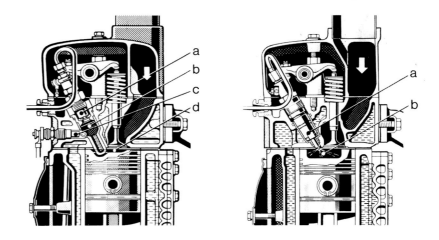

Left: Cross section of the pre-chamber diesel engine, OM322, 126 hp. **a,** injection nozzle. **b,** pre-chamber. **c,** glow plug. **d,** main combustion chamber (shallow recess in piston head). **Right:** Diesel engine with direct injection, OM352, 126 hp. **a,** injection nozzle. **b,** entire combustion chamber (deep recess in piston head).

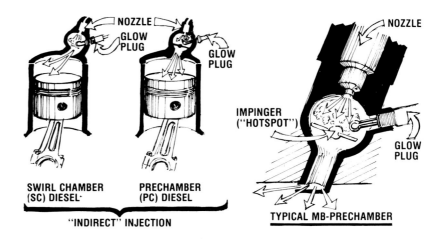

Injection systems for diesel engines

correspond to a three-liter diesel engine, and for identical torque a two-liter gasoline engine would correspond to a two-and-a-half-liter diesel engine.

Thus, a three-liter diesel engine has about the same horsepower output as a two-liter gasoline engine, but its torque is about 20 percent higher. If such a large diesel engine is selected for output compensation purposes, its weight and first cost (already higher) would be all the more higher. Greater weight and first cost of a comparable diesel engine, therefore, are due to increased displacement, higher engine rigidity, and the complexity of the injection system. A three-liter diesel engine is suitably a five-cylinder engine, while a two-liter gasoline engine always has four cylinders.

Although the pre-chamber engine has the lowest noise level of all possible diesel engine types, it is still higher than that of a gasoline engine in certain operating ranges, such as idling. However, the interior noise level in a pre-chamber diesel engined vehicle can be practically as low as that of a gasoline engine over most of the operating range.

Summing up, the relative drawbacks of the diesel engine are mainly, first, lower output and torque (from equal displacement); second, greater weight; third, higher first cost; and fourth, only marginally higher exterior noise level in the case of the pre-chamber diesel engine, definitely higher immediately after a cold start.

The biggest advantage of the diesel engine is its superior fuel economy. For example, in the 1974 model year the urban fuel economy of the 240 diesel model, in miles per gallon, was 70 percent better than the average vehicle weight class. And even with the improved economy of the new 1975 gasoline models, the much more powerful 300D has a 50 percent better economy than the gasoline average of this weight class. In addition to this, diesel fuel is commonly cheaper than premium or lead-free fuel in terms of cost per gallon, because it is cheaper to refine, similar to oil used for home heating purposes. So, for the diesel customers the real fuel economy in terms of cents per mile is unbeatably good.

For the model year 1975, a gasoline vehicle of the average 3,500 pound class got 15 miles per gallon in urban driving at a cost of 55 cents per gallon and the fuel cost per mile was 3.7 cents (equal to 100 percent); the diesel engined 240D and the 300D model got 24 miles per gallon in urban driving at a cost of 50 cents per gallon and the fuel cost per mile was 2.1 cents (equal to 57 percent).

In engineering circles one generally speaks in terms of specific fuel consumption or actual thermal efficiency. Actual thermal efficiency of an engine is rated in percent and represents that part of the total heat or energy contained in the consumed fuel which is actually turned into usable effective mechanical work or output. The rest is wasted, mostly in form of radiated and exhausted heat. Thermal efficiency values differ largely for one and the same engine, depending upon the air-fuel ratio, and so on, at the particular operating condition. They are notably lower than the theoretical values of an idealized engine, mentioned earlier.

Typical values, in actual thermal efficiency (percent) are, at full load and at medium speed of a passenger car gasoline engine 26 percent, and of a passenger car diesel engine (indirect injection) 30 percent; at part load and at medium speed of a passenger car gasoline engine 29 percent, and of a diesel engine 33 percent; and at low load and at low speed of a gasoline engine 13-20 percent, and of a diesel engine 20-25 percent. These figures should not be regarded as absolutes. They merely intend to be indicative for purposes of comparing actual efficiencies.

Some diesel antagonists fabricate all sorts of stories from the assertion that diesel fuel has more energy than gasoline. This is no precise statement and, strictly speaking, is not true. Energy contents of fuel depend upon the specific blend. On the average the energy content of diesel fuels is about the same as that of gasoline on a per-pound basis. But the diesel fuel quality in the United States varies much more widely than in Europe. Therefore, some diesel fuels have a lower energy content per pound, others a higher one. But diesel fuels always have a slightly higher density, so that a gallon of diesel fuel, on the average, will have a slightly higher heat content per gallon. This will not change the diesel engine's far superior efficiency. Moreover, diesel fuel is cheaper to refine. Gasoline fuel is refined with an additional energy input to end up with a fuel of high volatility but, on the average, with less energy content per gallon. So even in terms of fuel, diesel engines make a lot of sense, and we are not being wasteful if we produce and use diesel fuel.

The second big advantage of the diesel engine is its inherently low emission level. We understand this better if we recall what happens during the diesel engine's combustion. In the pre-chamber engine fuel is injected rather late, in fact, shortly before top dead center of the piston. Combustion is initiated by compression, and since the fuel is injected into the pre-chamber, combustion will first occur there. Since the pre-chamber has a very rich mixture, peak combustion temperatures will be relatively low. This leads to a low NO_x (oxides of nitrogen) formation.

Upon the descent of the piston, and as the pressure builds up due to the combustion in the pre-chamber, the partly oxidized fuel is forced into the main combustion chamber where it meets with a large surplus of air. Diesel engines always operate at large air excess ratios. Therefore, during this second phase of combustion, the lean mixture with a lot of oxygen results in a very thorough and complete burning process. Only very small quantities of unburned hydrocarbons (HC) and of carbon monoxide (CO), not completely oxidized to carbon dioxide, remain.

This very simple explanation is responsible for the low emission level of the diesel engine and, in fact the Mercedes-Benz passenger car diesel engines not only meet the pertaining standards of today (1974) but also those of 1977 without any engine modification or external gas treatment.

This now leads automatically to a number of other advantages. Since combustion is occuring at its optimum fuel economy, warm-up characteristics and driveability of the diesel engine are not impaired by emission regulations, at least not until model year 1977.

The third advantage of diesel-powered vehicles is engine durability. This point is a little difficult to explain. As we have seen, thermal and mechanical stresses in a diesel engine are higher than gasoline engine and the diesel engine has to be designed much more rigidly. In Europe, anyway, diesel engines have established a strong reputation for durabil-

ity. Some taxis run as much as 200,000 to 300,000 miles on one engine. Although taxi type of operation is not typical for common usage, the average diesel engine will last longer than the average gasoline engine, at least under European driving conditions.

Fourth, the maintenance and operating costs of diesel-engined vehicles are much lower than for gasoline-powered vehicles. This is particularly true for modern gasoline engines on the market, the maintenance cost of which has increased due to the complexity of the engine-emission control system. For a diesel customer the total cost aspects are altogether positive, because he can more than balance the higher first cost by the lower operational cost. We are, of course, comparing identical vehicles, say a Mercedes-Benz diesel with a Mercedes-Benz gasoline vehicle. The more the operator drives his car, the better his individual cost advantage will become. For the salesman, on the other hand, selling a diesel is a very special art and takes a rational approach, for he has to convince the potential customer to spend extra money for the purchase of his diesel vehicle and get across to him the conviction that due to the much lower operating cost this is altogether a wise buy.

Summing up, the relative advantages of diesel engines are, first, much better fuel economy; second, better average durability; third, lower emissions, without complicated add-on devices; fourth, due to lack of emission control devices ideal warm-up and driveability features; fifth, lower operating cost; and finally, lower total cost, if compared to an identical vehicle with gasoline engine.

Pollution and Emission Controls

Having mentioned air pollution, it might be beneficial to review the problem here briefly. Gasoline engines were heavily burdened to reduce air pollutants with emission equipment — air pumps, exhaust gas circulating systems, spark advance controls, deceleration valves, catalytic reactors, and other often expensive and complex devices, which caused many amazing and frustrating problems, but especially poor engine running particularly when first started. Diesel engines, on the other hand, did not need any devices and met all current standards of the U.S. government on allowable levels of pollutants, carbon monoxide (CO), hydrocarbons (HC), and oxides of nitrogen (NOx).

Carbon monoxide (CO) is an odorless, tasteless gas. If breathed in concentrated form it can be deadly. It is well known that CO is a major ingredient of the exhaust from gasoline engines, and people have been warned against running automobile engines in closed garages. Carbon monoxide can only be formed in a combustion environment in which there is a shortage of oxygen, but since a diesel engine runs inherently lean, the high air-fuel ratio actually provides an overabundance of oxygen for combustion, thus CO levels in diesel exhaust are extremely low.

Unburned hydrocarbons (HC) are simply parts of fuel that did not get completely burned during the combustion process. This happens much more frequently in a gasoline engine than in a diesel. Unlike in the diesel engine, the fuel of the gasoline engine enters the cylinder already mixed with its ration of air and is compressed in the cylinder in that form.

However, there is not necessarily an equal air-fuel charge in each cylinder because the complexities of intake manifold design make it virtually impossible to equally distribute the fuel from a centrally located carburetor to a number of cylinders located at varying distances from the carburetor. Before combustion takes place, some cylinders contain too much fuel for perfect combustion and others contain too little fuel. The direct cylinder fuel injection of the diesel engine assures an equal amount of fuel in each cylinder.

As the air and fuel are compressed in a gasoline engine's cylinder, tiny droplets of fuel tend to cling to the cylinder wall and the far recesses of the combustion chamber. Then, when the spark plug ignites the air-fuel mixture, the resulting flame front is not of sufficient size or duration to burn all the fuel hiding in these quench areas. When the exhaust valve opens, all this unburned fuel (HC) is forced out of the cylinder, through the exhaust pipe into the atmosphere. The HC emissions from diesel engines are generally lower because fuel does not enter the cylinder until the precise moment of combustion.

The lower air-fuel ratio of the gasoline engine also means that there is more fuel in the cylinder in relation to air, and thus less available oxygen, to support complete combustion.

Oxides of nitrogen (NOx) are a group of air pollutants which result from the chemical reaction taking place in the combustion chamber of the engine and the high temperature at which the reaction takes place. Theoretically, the way to deal with NOx levels is to lower the temperature at which combustion takes place. Automotive engineers, working on the modification of gasoline engines for low exhaust emissions, have found that indeed NOx levels could be lowered by lowering the engine operating and combustion chamber temperatures.

But the problem with this approach is that although a reduction in temperature decreases NOx, it also reduces the overall combustion efficiency of the engine. And any reduction in efficiency generally raises the quantities of carbon monoxide (CO) and of hydrocarbons (HC). It is a near classic case of robbing Peter to pay Paul, and the problem has caused tremendous difficulties in the design of clean gasoline engines.

The duration of the burning cycle in a diesel engine's combustion chamber is fortunately quite short, and the temperature at which diesel fuel burns is sufficiently low, and lower than that of gasoline. As a result, NOx emmissions from diesel engines are low enough at the present time to meet current federal exhaust emission standards without requiring any modifications.

The Environmental Protection Agency set the following emission standards for light-duty diesel vehicles for the years indicated:

	HC (Hydrocarbon)	CO (Carbon Monoxide)	NOx (Oxides of Nitrogen)
1975	1.5	15.0	3.1
1977-1979	1.5	15.0	2.0
1980	.41	7.0	2.0
1981	.41	3.4	1.0

In 1975 test results were:

(Federal test)	Weight	Axle ratio	HC	CO	NOx
Mercedes-Benz 220D			.34	1.24	1.43
(California test) 240D	3,500	3.69	0.2	1.2	1.3
240D	3,500	3.69	0.1	1.0	1.4
300D	3,500	3.46	0.2	1.4	1.6

For the 1977 model year:

(Federal test)					
Mercedes-Benz 240D	3,500	3.69	0.2	2.0	1.6
240D	3,500	3.69	0.4	1.0	1.6
240D	3,500	3.69	0.4	1.0	1.4
300D	4,000	3.46	0.3	1.0	1.7
300D	4,000	3.46	0.5	1.0	1.8

In 1979 the Environmental Protection Agency proposed that the emission goals for 1981 were to be 0.6 grams per mile of particulate matter. Mercedes-Benz diesel passenger cars were tested and showed that the 240D had 0.36 grams, the 300D had 0.41 grams, and the 300SD had 0.45 grams per mile. All were considerably below that requirement. For 1983 the proposals were to be considerably stricter, calling for 0.2 grams per mile of particulate matter. In the opinion of expert emission engineers such a limit would actually be impossible to attain and would mean the end of diesel automobiles in this country. However, indications were that these stringent goals would be postponed to 1985.

But in California, the emission control regulations for 1980 required a NOx limit of 1.0 gram per mile for cars, guaranteeing 50,000

miles durability, or 1.5 grams for a guarantee of 100,000 miles. Still stricter emission control requirements were expected to come.

The 1980 model year 300CD cars, as well as all 300 line diesels, carried the two stickers: A silver colored label on the door jamb read:

> **Vehicle Emission Control Information**
> **This vehicle conforms to U.S.E.P.A.**
> **Regulations applicable to 1980 model year**
> **New motor vehicles**
> **NON CATALYST**
> **123 584 8121**

A black label with white printing, placed on the front body plate under the hood read:

> **Vehicle Emission Control Information Daimler-Benz A.G. Stuttgart-Untertuerkheim**
> **Displacement: 2998 cm³. Engine family: 80.21.35.30. Approved M.B. Emission Control System: DFI.** **Initial injection:**
> **24 Deg. BTDC. Idle - RPM: 750 ± 50. Mfr. adjusted. Transmission in neutral. Accessories not in operation. Advertised Horsepower: 83 HP.**
> **Fuel Rate at adv. Horsepower: 40.5 mm³/stroke. Valve lash at water temp. below 30°C: Intake 0.10 mm, Exhaust 0.30 mm.**
> **Valve lash at water temp. Above 45°C: Intake 0.15 mm. Measured between rocker arm pad and cam.**
> **This vehicle conforms to U.S. EPA Regulations applicable to 1980 model year New Motor Vehicles.**
> **123 548 88 21**

The official fuel EPA consumption ratings for highway (hy), city (cy) and combined (cb) were for:

	1979 hy-cy-cb	1980 hy-cy-cb	(California) hy-cy-cb	1981 hy-cy-cb
240D (manual)	34-30-32	34-28-30		33-29-31
240D (automatic)	31-27-29	29-26-27		31-27-29
300D/300CD	28-23-25	28-23-25	28-24-26	28-24-26
300TD	28-23-25	28-23-25	28-24-26	30-26-28
300SD	29-24-26	32-24-27	31-24-27	30-26-28

EXHAUST EMISSIONS – AIR POLLUTION – EMISSION CONTROL

Under favourable conditions, the exhaust of an internal combustion engine contains primarily carbon dioxide (CO_2) and water vapor. Depending on engine load (idle, partial throttle or full throttle) and operating temperature, small quantities of other gases may be produced. These are, specifically: unburned hydrocarbons (HC), carbon monoxide (CO) and oxides of nitrogen (NOx) – as well as black smoke (soot) with diesel engines. In the interests of maintaining clean air, the amount of these emissions should be as low as possible.

The diesel engine performs very well in regard to exhaust emissions, since it attains nearly complete burning of the fuel. Therefore, the exhaust of a diesel engine contains only very small quantities of undesirable substances. Visible diesel smoke (opacity), which can sometimes be observed, may be perhaps optically annoying. Technically speaking, it cannot be eliminated completely in all cases. However, with diesel engines of modern design which are properly maintained, this happens only very rarely. The fuel injection pump, the governor and the combustion chamber determine primarily the mixture-formation and the quality of the combustion in a diesel engine.

The fuel pump which is driven by the injection pump, draws the fuel from the fuel tank through the pre-filter and forces it through the fuel main filter into the suction chamber of the injection pump.

The four (engine 616) or five (engine 617) injection pump plungers push the fuel in the suction chamber over the pressure check valve into the pressure line to the injection nozzle.

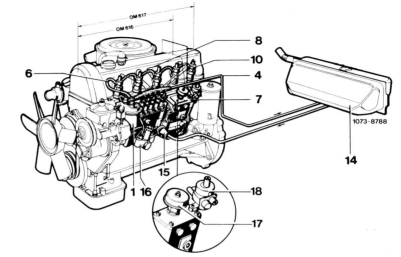

Diesel Engine Fuel System

1 Fuel main filter
4 Fuel return line to tank
6 Fuel return line from injection nozzles
7 Injection pump
8 High pressure line to nozzles
10 Injection nozzle
14 Fuel tank
15 Fuel pre-filter
16 Fuel pump with hand pump
17 Automatic altitude compensator
18 Vacuum control valve (only vehicles with automatic transmission)

Injection Timing Device

1 Drive sprocket with primary segment plate
2 Fly weights
3 Secondary segment plate
4 Drive flange with face cam for vacuum pump
5 Stretch bolt
6 Bushing
7 Thrust washer
8 Bushing
10 Spring seat
11 Compression spring
12 Stop pin (limit for timing range)

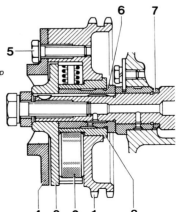
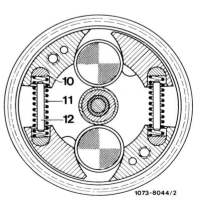

From the 1980 Owner's Manual for 240D, 300D, 300CD and 300TD

Mercedes-Benz Pre-Chamber Principle

From the nozzle, the fuel is injected into the pre-chamber and the main combustion chamber.

The Mercedes-Benz passenger car diesel engines function according to the Mercedes-Benz pre-chamber principle. With this principle, the diesel fuel is injected into the pre-chamber at the moment of highest compression. From there, the burning fuel-air mixture is forced through 6 narrow passages into the main combustion chamber. This creates an intensive swirling action and therefore a uniform and complete combustion is obtained. The Mercedes-Benz Pre-Chamber Diesel Engines have a relatively low noise level.

A precisely metered amount of fuel delivered at the proper instant is also important for proper mixture-formation in a diesel engine. The amount of fuel to be injected is determined by the fuel injection pump and the governor which control the fuel quantity depending on engine speed and engine load. In addition, the governor limits the fuel delivery when maximum permissible engine revolutions are reached. The moment of fuel injection is regulated by an automatic

injection timing device which advances the point of fuel injection with increasing engine-rpm's so that even at higher rpm's sufficient time for proper combustion is available.

To meet regulated emission levels also at higher altitudes, the fuel injection pumps are equipped with an automatic altitude compensation system.

The factory-determined settings of the fuel injection pump, as well as the design of the governor and the injection timing device, yield optimal fuel combustion.

If these settings are not adhered to at maintenance inspections or if nonpermissible modifications are made on emission related components, this will adversely affect the exhaust emissions. It is the responsibility of the vehicle owner that no adjustments and modifications are made to his Mercedes-Benz Model 240 D, 300 D, 300 CD or 300 TD.

In addition, we feel obligated to point out that it is legally not permissible to alter the function of emission related components.

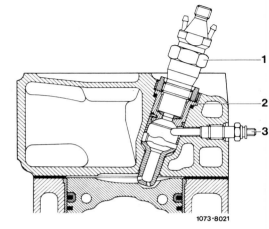

1073-8021

1 Injection nozzle
2 Pre-chamber
3 Pin-type glow plug

Exhaust Gas Recirculation (EGR)

"Applicable Only to Vehicles Equipped Accordingly".

To reduce nitric oxides (NOx) in the exhaust gases, a portion of the exhaust gas is recirculated into the intake manifold.

Above 17° C/62° F coolant temperature, and according to engine load, vacuum is applied to the diaphragm of the EGR valve depending on the position of the switch-over valve (64) and the modulator vacuum control valve (65). The EGR valve is opened. Depending on the position of the EGR valve diaphragm, exhaust gas is routed from the exhaust manifold to the intake manifold. There they are mixed with the intake air and drawn into the combustion chambers.

Functional Schematic

 1 Intake manifold
31 Exhaust manifold
36 Thermo-vacuuum valve 17° C/62° F
60 EGR Valve
61 Corrugated metal tube
62 Orifice in T-fitting
63 Orifice in connection fitting
64 Switch-over valve
65 Vacuum control valve
66 Fuel injection pump
67 Vacuum pump
68 Control linkage lever with cam

a To automatic transmission
b Vent line into passenger compartment
c To brake booster

bk = black   wh = white
br = brown   gr = green
pu = purple re = red

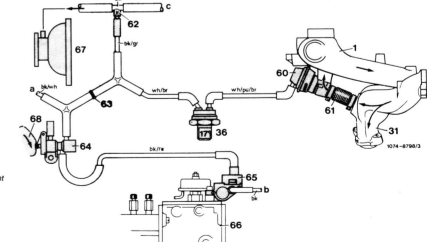

1074-8798/3

From the 1980 Owner's Manual for 240D, 300D, 300CD and 300TD

148

Crankcase Ventilation

The engines 616 and 617 (without EGR) are equipped with a maintenance free, positive crankcase ventilation system.

The vapors and condensate are drawn directly from the cylinder head cover into the intake manifold and from there into the combustion chambers.

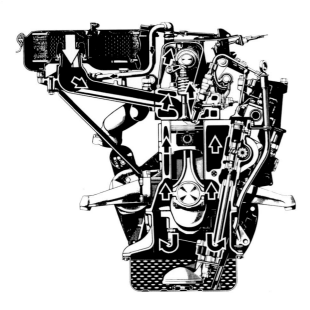

⇦ Fresh air
◀ Blow-by gases

Crankcase Ventilation

The engine 617 (with EGR) is equipped with a maintenance free, positive crankcase ventilation system.

The engine blow-by gases and crankcase vapors are drawn via the vent insert (1), which is riveted to the cylinder head cover and the connection fitting (2) to the cyclone oil seperator (3) in the air filter housing. There, the gases are mixed with the intake air and routed to the combustion chambers.

The oil collected in the oil cyclone separator (3) flows through the return line (6) and the check valve (7) installed in the upper oil pan housing, back into the oil pan.

The check valve prevents that crankcase vapors from the oil pan are drawn into the air intake system due to the existing vacuum.

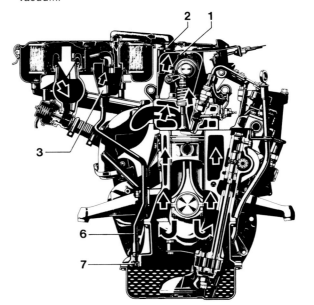

1 Vent insert
2 Connection fitting
3 Oil separator
6 Return line
7 Check valve
⇦ Fresh air
◀ Blow-by gases

From the 1980 Owner's Manual for 240D, 300D, 300CD and 300TD

149

Turbocharger

Model 300 SD is equipped with a turbocharger. The turbocharger is an exhaust gas driven compressor mounted on the exhaust manifold. It consists of a turbine, a center housing with bearings and seals, as well as a compressor, which is connected via a common shaft to the turbine.

The turbine is driven by the velocity of the exhaust gases. The turbocharger speed is dependent on the flow rate of the exhaust gases, and can obtain maximum speeds up to approx. 100,000 rpm.

At idle speed, the engine operates as a normally aspirated engine. With increasing load and rpm, the ·compressor impeller begins to produce boost pressure.

The supercharged air is then delivered via the intake manifold to the individual cylinders. This achieves a better charging of the cylinders, improved combustion and, simultaneously, an increase in engine performance.

The amount of fuel to be injected is continously varied depending on the existing air pressure in the intake manifold thereby achieving an optimum fuel/air ratio for combustion.

It is the responsibility of the vehicle owner that no adjustments and modifications are made to his Mercedes-Benz Model 300 SD.

In addition, we feel obligated to point out that it is legally not permissible to alter the function of emission related components.

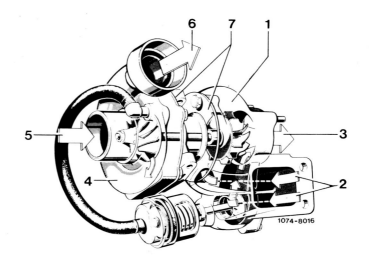

1074-8016

Turbocharger

1 Turbine
2 Exhaust gas inlet
3 Exhaust gas discharge
4 Compressor
5 Ambient air inlet
6 Compressed air discharge
7 Center housing

From the 1979 Owner's Emission Control and Maintenance Manual for 300SD